Published by John Wiley & Sons, Inc., Hoboken, New Jersey
Published simultaneously in Canada

For general information about our other products and services, please contact our Customer Care Department within the United States at (800) 762-2974 or outside the United States at (317) 572-3993, or fax (317) 572-4002.

Wiley also publishes its books in a variety of electronic formats. Some content that appears in print may not be available in electronic books. For more information about Wiley products, visit our Web site at www.wiley.com.

Library of Congress Cataloging-in-Publication Data:

Klimchuk, Marianne Rosner
Packaging Design: Successful Product Branding from Concept to Shelf /
Marianne Rosner Klimchuk, Sandra A. Krasovec.
    p. cm.
  Includes bibliographical references and index.
  ISBN-13: 978-0-471-72016-4 (cloth)
  ISBN-10: 0-471-72016-X (cloth)
  1. Packaging--Design. I. Krasovec, Sandra A. II. Title.

  TS195.4.K65 2006
  658.5'64--dc22

                              2006004539
Printed in the United States of America

10 9 8 7 6 5 4 3 2 1

Design: raisedBarb Graphics
Cover: Sandra A. Krasovec, Marianne Rosner Klimchuk, and Robert Ludemann

PACKAGINGDESIGN

PACKAGINGDESIGN

Successful Product Branding from Concept to Shelf

Marianne Rosner Klimchuk and Sandra A. Krasovec

WILEY

John Wiley & Sons, Inc.

CONTENTS

CHAPTER 9   PLANNING FOR PRODUCTION   165

CHAPTER 10   THE DESIGN PROCESS   183

CHAPTER 11 CONSIDERING THE ENVIRONMENT 221

CHAPTER 12 UNDERSTANDING LEGAL ISSUES 231

Acknowledgments

Many talented and generous people have contributed both directly and indirectly to making *Packaging Design: Successful Product Branding from Concept to Shelf* a reality. The business of packaging design brought the authors together more than 16 years ago and our professional bond continues with ever-expanding opportunities and ventures. We are forever indebted to our packaging design students; over the years each and every one of them have contributed to this book and have educated us in ways that are immeasurable. We are grateful to our academic colleagues — outstanding design professionals in their own right — including the late László Roth, Suzanne Anoushian, Bob Avino, Cliff Bachner, Frank Csoka, Sondra Graff, Marcus Hewitt, Susan Hewitt, Joan Nicosia, Michael Pace, Barbara Rietschel, Jack Schecterson, Adam Straus, Peter Weber, Barbara Wentz, George Wybenga, and countless others. Their professional knowledge and superb teaching skills have greatly influenced many aspects of this book. We thank our design colleagues at the many firms and corporations who have opened their doors to us, guest lectured, answered our endless e-mails, and contributed their outstanding work, philosophy, and professional process to this book; they have been generous with their time and expertise, which has been a valuable resource of information, and their work is truly inspirational. Special thanks to Sondra Graff for her initial design inspiration, and to Barbara Rietschel for her expertise in shepherding us through book design and production files in record time. Thank you to Margaret Cummins for the direction and guidance of two novices throughout the entire process, and to Leslie Anglin for her production assistance. Thank you to our friends who have endured this long process with us and have been our tireless supporters.

We dedicate this book to our families. Their appreciation for packaging design, evidenced by their own discerning consumer purchases, has deepened our infatuation with these physical objects and the role they play in our lives as educators, designers, and consumers. Edward and Constance Krasovec and Lydia and Jonathan Rosner; and Karen, Deb, Bryan, Alex, Ashley, Nicholas, Ed, Amanda, Andrew, Jake, Laura, Pat, Art, Beth, Josh, Glenn, Christa, Niki, and Noah have all been supportive and enthusiastic about this major endeavor. Most importantly, without the love, support, patience, and endless encouragement of Stephen Yip, and Garth, Aaron and Sasha Klimchuk this book would not have become a reality.

Foreword

The strength of television advertising as the primary communication with consumers has been dramatically reduced by the increase of media options and the consumer's ability to "zap" TV commercials. Marketers who are looking for new ways to get their message to consumers while getting more value for the dollars they spend, recognize that packaging can be the key tool to communicate their brand to the consumer.

While good packaging design is key to creating a successful brand, there is far more to packaging design than designing logos and graphics. A successful packaging design requires an understanding of the consumer, knowledge of current and future trends, and a solid grasp of the competitive shelf set. In addition to the written message, packaging design needs to express the brand promise and brand personality that make an emotional connection with the consumer at the time the purchase decision is being made at shelf. AG Lafley, CEO of Proctor & Gamble has effectively labeled this interaction with the consumer as the "First Moment of Truth".

To successfully position your brand during this "First Moment of Truth", it is important to create a comprehensive brief and to plan realistic timelines. Following the correct order of events in building a brand saves time and money and provides a more effective and successful end result. Very few people or companies understand the total process of creating a brand and its packaging as well as the authors do here.

Marianne Rosner Klimchuck and Sandra A. Krasovec have created an in-depth guide to positioning your brand, understanding your consumer and setting objectives prior to creating the brand image. Their clearly defined step-by-step information is thorough, easy to understand and easy to use both by those within the industry and others needing to understand the process. Anyone interested in using packaging design to enhance a brand will find in this book what they need to know to be effective.

Pamela Parisi
Director, Global Design Resources
The Gillette Company
Proctor & Gamble

Preface

The primary goal of *Packaging Design: Successful Product Branding from Concept to Shelf* is to serve as a guide for manufacturers, marketers, design firms (packaging, brand, advertising, graphic, and industrial design), researchers, product developers, printers, and any other professionals involved in the world of consumer branding. Faculty and students in disciplines such as packaging and graphic design, marketing and communications, advertising, display and exhibit design, product development, manufacturing, and industrial design and engineering should all find this book an invaluable resource. Consumers may also find the process of getting a product to retail enlightening since most have no idea of the complexity of developing a product and its packaging design.

This book details the professional roles and design methodology, providing an understanding of how packaging designs are developed and how they function as the marketing vehicle for consumer products. A condensed historical overview provides a sense of perspective for the business of packaging design as we know it today. The chapters define the visual elements, design principles, and processes from concept to production, consumer marketing strategies, and legal, environmental, and global issues that significantly impact packaging design. The successful marketing of consumer products hinges on the packaging design; herein more than 300 images include typographic studies, illustrations of concept sketches, design development, primary display panels, packaging redesigns, and case studies that demonstrate designs that stand out from the competition. The text also includes anecdotes, design pointers, and calendars that reflect a typical week in the life of an industry professional.

The authors, full-time faculty members at the Fashion Institute of Technology (FIT), the only institution in the United States that offers a BFA degree in packaging design, have a combined 25 years of academic experience and 35 years in the profession. They have worked on packaging design assignments for beverages and food as well as pharmaceutical, personal care, and household products, to name a few. Using their extensive experience and global industry contacts, they have been able to provide a comprehensive viewpoint on the business of packaging design.

1 ACCOUNTING FOR THE PAST

Developments through Emerging Societies

The history of packaging design is inextricably linked to every aspect of the emerging
cultures of humankind. Developments in technology, materials, production, and
the conditions of evolving consumer societies carved the need for packaging to
protect, store, and transport goods. Packaging design became the means to visually
communicate the product contents. This condensed historical perspective explores
how advancements of civilizations, growth of trade among people, human discoveries,
technological inventions, and countless global events helped to facilitate the birth and
evolution of packaging design.

Packaging design's prehistory began with people's need for possessions, and as early
as 8000 BC natural materials such as woven grasses and cloths, bark, leaves, shells,
clay pottery, and crude glassware were used to make containers for holding goods.
Hollow vegetable gourds and animal bladders were the precursors to glass bottles, and
animal skins and leaves were the forerunners to paper bags and plastic wrap.

The basic ideas of commerce were founded on trade between early civilizations.
Natural goods harvested for a variety of uses were indigenous to particular areas; other
goods were introduced as products by specific tribes or societies. In either case, as

Funerary Urn
Italy (Etruscan)
9th–7th century
BC. Volcanic clay.
h: 46.5 cm (18
5/16 in.) Cooper-
Hewitt, National
Design Museum,
Smithsonian
Institution. Gift
of Karen Johnson
Keland, 1976-
102-1

people traveled the world, demand was created for goods that were only available in specific places. As cultures developed and became less nomadic, the trading of goods became the forerunner to *economics*, the science of the distribution and consumption of goods.

Capitalism through the Ages

In both capitalistic and economic principles the object is the fundamental unit of value. Capitalistic societies, similar to the early mercantile ones, rely on the creation of a consumer culture in which a large segment of society does not produce most of what it consumes. Capitalism therefore is based essentially on the distribution of goods—moving them from one place to another. In developed societies where people no longer interact with those that make objects they consume and the only relation they have is with the object itself, the product becomes highly valued. Consumers define themselves by what they purchase rather than what they produce.

Dating back to the Middle Ages, the earliest forms of mercantile society in China, Rome, and the Middle East were defined by the distribution of goods for profit. As people made their way throughout the world, goods were transported greater distances and so there was a considerable need for vessels to carry the goods. The spice trade in 330, the drinking of coffee in 500, and the growing wine industry in 800 indicated that in these early economies items were shared and bartered not only among neighbors but were also carried by traders from village to village and beyond. The Silk Road trade route between Asia and Europe made it possible for goods to be delivered from one side of the continent to the other. The crossroads of such routes mixed cultures and religions, and the variety of goods that were traded needed to be contained.

By 750 there was widespread use of bottles, jars, and urns made of earthenware. Skilled artisans handcrafted ceramic containers and other decorative receptacles to house incense, perfumes, and ointments.

Group of Vessels
Roman Empire,
probably Syria,
1st–4th century.
Glass.
h: 17.5 cm (6 7/8
in.) (tallest pictured)
Cooper-Hewitt,
National Design
Museum, Smithsonian
Institution. Gifts
of Rodman
Wanamaker, 1919-24-
33,39,41,44,55,70,
and Mrs. Leo
Wallerstein, 1959-
114-2 (second
from right).

Industrialization of
the glassmaking
process in the
first century
resulted in the use
of hollow glass
vessels as perfume
receptacles.

Societal upheavals with religious and economic powers vying for control throughout civilizations of the world—such as the Crusades (1096–1291)—sped the development of trade routes between the Orient and the West. Crusaders brought back scents, spices, and other exotic goods, spurring the growth of trade and the need for a wider variety of packaging to serve as containment and protection. Commercial materials slowly replaced natural containers.

History of Writing

The business of packaging design as we know it was spawned by visually identifying products through pictorial representation. Sumerian marks or pictographs enabled communication to advance from a spoken language to a written one, allowing messages to last through time. These pictures evolved into syllabic symbols and became a form of communication used by many cultures for almost 2,000 years. With the Phoenician development of single-sound symbols, the alphabet became the visual foundation for the evolution of written languages.

Early symbols were the forerunners to trademarks or brand names. These symbols evolved from the need or desire to establish identification in three ways: social identity (who is it), ownership (who owns it), and origin (who made it).

With written communication came the need for writing surfaces. From 500 BC to 170 BC papyrus rolls (the word *paper* is derived from the *papyrus*, which was a plant found in Egypt), and early parchments made of dried reeds developed into the first portable writing surfaces. The earliest papers found in the world were produced in China in approximately 105. Ts'ai Lun, an official of the imperial court of the Han Emperor Ho-di, is credited as the first papermaker.

Researchers discovered that the Western Han Dynasty used these papers for not only for writing but for wallpaper, toilet paper, napkins, and wrapping used for packaging. Papermaking evolved over the next 1,500 years, reaching the Middle East and spreading across Europe about 750 and west to the United Kingdom in 1310. Papermaking techniques reached America in the late 1600s.

Within some 800 years sociological, cultural, political, and economic developments dramatically changed history. The merchant classes developed in the twelfth and thirteenth centuries as a social and economic group functioning to move product from one locale to another. Buying and selling goods became a way to make a living, rather than farming or producing objects and other material necessities. Along with this new class came a rising interest in the outside world and a demand for goods from faraway places. The written word on paper gave way to modern printing.

Early Symbols
The Greeks took the letters of the Phoenician alphabet and turned them into beautiful art forms, standardizing each with component vertical and horizontal strokes based on geometric constructions. This marked the beginning of letterform design.

Printing

Printing is thought to have begun in China with the first wooden printing presses, invented there in 305 BC, and movable clay type, in 1041. In 1200 tinplate iron was developed in Bohemia and printing took hold throughout Europe. In approximately 1450 Johannes Gutenberg was credited for inventing the printing press. This workable press, with movable and replaceable wooden or metal letters, brought together the technologies of paper, oil-based ink, and the winepress to print books. The Gutenberg press was not a single invention but the entirety of many technologies developed centuries before. With its movable type, it contributed to lowering the price of printed materials and making them available to the masses, leading to the rapid increase in demand for paper and sparking a revolution in mass communication.

THE TERM *TYPEFACE*

The original term *typography* refers to the style or appearance of printed matter and the process of printing from type. Independent, movable, and reusable, pieces of metal with raised letterforms on top were called hot metal or foundry type. Each piece was cast into a precise size and contained a raised image of a single letter, number, or other character. The block of metal that carried the raised image was the body. The raised image that was inked for printing was the face, from which we get the term *typeface*.

The Beginnings of Visual Communication

Out of the transition from the medieval to the modern world, the rebirth period of the Renaissance, emerged the concept of graphic design. The innovation of book design brought around developments such as beautiful typographic styles, illustrations, ornaments, and page layouts that followed into other forms of visual communication.

In the mid-1500s Andreas Bernhart, who owned a paper mill, and other early German papermakers were among the first tradesmen to put their names on their products with printed wrappers. Bernhart's wrappers became the means of merchandising paper products by decorating them with printed designs. These wrappers are among the earliest records of packaging design.

The use of billboards and "broadsides"—announcements posted on sides of buildings to post laws and government decrees—marked the first forms of advertising. Later advertising was a vehicle to depict early packaging design. In early British newspapers, vendors posted or "advertised" products such as medicine bottles with printed labels and illustrated tobacco wrappers. Packaging design evolved with the idea that the visual experience provided by the package was a critical component to sales.

As design disciplines grew out of the need to communicate information in visually graphic form, they melded with the material wants and needs of everyday life. With cheaper and more abundant merchandise, the growth of trade advanced the need for a wider variety of packaging that served to provide greater protection and preservation of goods. In essence, the combination of the physical container or package and the written communication about the goods contained became the foundation for packaging design today.

Industrialization

Eighteenth-century Europe was a time of great commercial expansion with the rapid growth of cities and the broader distribution of wealth from the affluent down to the working class. Technological advancements spurred production cycles to keep up with the increased population. Mass production provided goods that were readily available at lower costs.

The concern for hygiene within the growing bourgeois society gave rise to the emergence of two spaces in the home: the toilet and the bathroom. Thus the market for personal-care products expanded, and packaging design for soaps and other bath products reflected these new luxurious values.

Tea Packaging Illustrations
1800 Woodcuts by Thomas Bewick and His School. Edited by Blanche Cirker and editorial staff. 1962. New York: Dover Publications Inc.

In 1559, tea was introduced in Europe and traders recognized the need to mark their names on their goods, provide information, and improve sales by making the product more visually appealing.

TOILET PAPER

Toilet paper, first produced in China in the fourteenth century, became a staple consumer product as indoor plumbing improved and the public's desire for better hygiene increased. New Yorker Joseph C. Gayetty produced the first packaged bathroom tissue in the United States in 1857. The Gayetty firm, in New Jersey, produced "The Therapeutic Paper," which contained aloe as a curative ingredient. The company sold this product in packs of 500 sheets for 50 cents, and Joseph Gayetty's name was printed on each sheet.

In 1890 the Scott Paper Company was the first to manufacture the "unmentionable" product on rolls for use as toilet paper. Scott purchased large rolls from various paper mills and converted them into packages of small rolls and stacked sheets, customizing them for each of its merchant-customers.

With the success of this private-label business, the company began to concentrate on its own products. However, since toilet paper continued to be a sensitive subject for consumers, Scott purchased the private-label name "Waldorf" from the Waldorf Hotel and began producing this as their first branded product. As acceptance grew with consumers, the company branded its own Scott® toilet tissue, which by 1925 was the leading toilet paper in the world. Kimberly Clark bought the Scott Paper Company in 1995.

Original Scott Toilet Paper
Photo: Ian House, American Package Museum, www.packagemuseum.com

The packaging design and secondary copy "Soft as old Linen" evokes the linen needlepoint towels of the period.

Product development increased to meet consumer wants and needs in a flourishing society. Packaging design for products—such as bottled beers and antidotes, pots of snuff, bottled fruits, mustards, pins, tobacco, tea, and powders—functioned to identify the manufacturer and communicate about the product's purpose.

Coats of arms were common graphic elements of early packaging design as they signified the family that manufactured the goods or provided a regional mark of distinction. These symbols are frequently used in packaging designs today, particularly in the beer and spirits categories, to communicate authenticity, heraldry, tradition, and trustworthiness.

Old Coats of Arms
1800 Woodcuts by Thomas Bewick and His School. Edited by Blanche Cirker and editorial staff. 1962. New York: Dover Publications Inc.

Historically, heraldic imagery was ornate, detailed, and often included images of uniquely powerful animals such as lions, unicorns, and dragons.

Chivas Regal Tins
Client: Pernod Ricard
Design Firm: Webb
Scarlett deVlam
Creative Director:
Felix Scarlett (below)
Designers:
Sara Fagan,
Sophie Reynolds

THE CHIVAS STORY

With this range of tins for Chivas Regal Premium Blended Old Scotch Whiskey, Webb Scarlett de Vlam chose to use imagery that was rooted in brand truth and heritage yet abstractly communicated emotional values. Two series of tin designs used on the Chivas Regal carton explore the classic heraldic imagery.

As Felix Scarlett states, the first packaging design series used objects created by the traditional heraldic craftsmen still found in Britain. The goal was to communicate, in a contemporary way, some of the historical reality and meaning behind what some consumers consider simply a decorated box. This idea was taken further on the second series, by identifying elements at the distillery that echoed aspects of this visual heritage and would enable the design to explore some of the emotional reward a Chivas drinker enjoys. The keys used in the design to illustrate the cross keys (heraldic meaning: the keys of St. Peter, representing household management, property, and education) were old distillery warehouse keys. This enabled the design to explore the idea of care, time, and aging. With each design the goal was to combine in one image a relevant emotion, product meaning, and heritage story rooted in the brand actuality.

By the 1740s America, as a British colony, imported most manufactured luxury goods from England, France, Holland, and Germany for a rather small population. There were only one million inhabitants in 1750, which grew to seven million by 1810. There was little inducement for most traders to print their names and addresses on their goods since most of the population could not read. Of the nine million inhabitants in Britain, only 80,000 were literate; it can be assumed that these were the customers buying consumer goods. Early packaging design was clearly designed for the affluent upper classes.

By the early 1800s as the population grew in Europe and America, barrels, wooden boxes, and jute sacks were widely used as packaging materials. With the greater demand for consumer goods, developments in tin, aluminum, glass, and paper bags emerged as significant resources for packaging.

THE INVENTION OF THE PAPER BAG

Francis Wolle invented and patented the first paper bag machine in the United States in 1852. He and his brother, along with other paper bag manufacturers, founded the Union Paper Bag Machine Company in 1869.

Working for the Columbia Paper Bag Company, employee Margaret Knight invented a new machine part to cut, fold, and paste square-bottomed paper bags. Before that bags had been more like envelopes. After a legal fight to protect her invention, she was awarded the patent in 1870. Called the mother of the paper bag, Knight founded the Eastern Paper Bag Company that same year and received patents for several other industrial machines.

Three important innovations came almost at the same time during the turn of the century.

- Invention of the papermaking machine
- Discovery of lithography
- Development of American packaging

The invention of the papermaking machine, in France in 1798 by Nicholas Louis Robert, allowed paper to be produced faster and at lower prices. The principle of this machine, to form paper on an endless belt, meant that the handmade process using separate molds was no longer required.

The mass industrialization of paper, started by the papermaking machine in Europe, hit the shores of the United States by the mid-1800s. The mechanized process of making paper was followed by the invention of machines that made paperboard. This opened up the world of paper, previously used for writing and communication, to paperboard for packaging.

In 1817 the first commercial paperboard box was produced in England, 200 years after the Chinese invented it, and emerged as a revolutionary development at the end of the nineteenth century. Paperboard packaging was commercially produced in 1839, and within ten years boxes for a wide assortment of products were being manufactured. Corrugated board appeared in the 1850s as a more durable secondary packaging material to ship many items together. As competition between manufacturers took off, specialized equipment was developed to speed production and reduce costs.

Robert Gair, an American printer in Brooklyn, invented the bulk manufacturing of paperboard boxes in 1890. Quite accidentally, when a metal ruler shifted out of place during a printing run, he discovered that by cutting and folding in one operation he could make prefabricated cartons. Around 1900 paperboard cartons began to replace self-made boxes and wooden crates used for trade. This marked the origin of the cereal box as we know it today. Box making and tin can manufacturing grew significantly both in America and England during the early 1900s. With the expansion of trade, machinery was needed not only to make boxes but also to weigh product contents, fill and seal them.

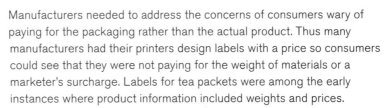

Manufacturers needed to address the concerns of consumers wary of paying for the packaging rather than the actual product. Thus many manufacturers had their printers design labels with a price so consumers could see that they were not paying for the weight of materials or a marketer's surcharge. Labels for tea packets were among the early instances where product information included weights and prices.

The "Original and Best" Kellogg's® Corn Flakes used paperboard cartons to hold flaked corn cereal. A heat-sealed waxed bag of Waxtite® was initially wrapped around the outside of the box and was printed with the brand name and product information. Later the Waxtite® was moved to inside the carton. The marketing of cereal through paperboard packaging was a clear depiction of Kellogg's strong understanding of the strength of their brand through the marriage of structure and visual brand elements that made up their packaging design.

**Early Quaker Oats
Paperboard Canister**
The Quaker Oats Company in the United States was one of the earlier companies that expanded the use of machinery to weigh out portions and fill paperboard cartons to market their products.

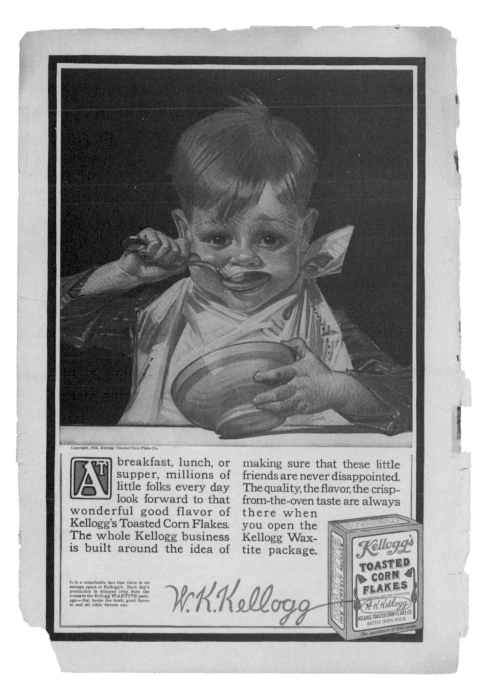

At breakfast, lunch, or supper, millions of little folks every day look forward to that wonderful good flavor of Kellogg's Toasted Corn Flakes. The whole Kellogg business is built around the idea of making sure that these little friends are never disappointed. The quality, the flavor, the crisp-from-the-oven taste are always there when you open the Kellogg Wax-tite package.

It is a remarkable fact that there is no storage space at Kellogg's. Each day's production is shipped crisp from the ovens in the Kellogg *WAXTITE* pack-age—that keeps the fresh, good flavor in and all other flavors out.

W. K. Kellogg

Kellogg's
TOASTED
CORN
FLAKES

Kellogg's Corn Flakes Waxtite Advertisement
The Ladies Home Journal, April 1916

Early Branding

As early as the mid-1800s manufacturers adopted the term of *brand*. This term derived from the use a hot branding iron to burn a distinctive mark into the hides of livestock in order for ranchers to claim them as rightful property. This idea of ownership communicated through a visual symbol became the means by which merchants and manufacturers guaranteed the promise of the quality of their goods by their "brand" symbol or name and provided the consumer a way to trace the product back to its source. The brand also became the vehicle for protecting the manufacturers' proprietary information about their products as well as a visual reminder to help consumers remember their brand.

SMITH BROTHERS

The Smith Brothers pioneered the official brand and "trademark" for their world-famous cough drops in Poughkeepsie, New York. First marketed in large glass jars in the mid-1800s, they needed to be differentiated from candies sold the same way. The brothers decided to put their own pictures on small envelopes supplied to shopkeepers to dole out cough drops to customers. Pictures of William with the word *Trade* underneath and Andrew with the word *Mark* underneath on the preprinted envelopes helped make their product a success. Their idea of using the packaging to "brand" the product was revolutionary. The business grew with the sons and grandsons of the Smith brothers continuing to mass-produce the product in a new automated factory built in 1915. As the packaging changed from envelopes to folding cartons, their "trademarked" pictures remained.

Branding Iron
(above)
Carefully crafted of metal, these instrumental tools served to distinguish owners of livestock.

Smith Brothers Cough Drops
(right)
Photo: Ian House, The American Package Museum, www.packagemuseum.com

This packaging with its trademark images of the two brothers was revolutionary for its time.

Lithography

The principle of lithography, discovered by Alois Senefelder in 1798, was a significant milestone in the history of packaging design and was advanced by the developments of mass production. Since everything from cardboard boxes, wooden crates, bottles, and tins had a paper label, the lithographic proces of printing labels was one of the notable developments of the time. Until then every label or wrapper was printed by hand with wooden presses on handmade paper. By the mid-1800s multiple-colored designs could be reproduced in large quantities. Wallpaper print techniques inspired by the current art period influenced the design of labels, boxes, and tins.

The Linotype (line of type) composing machine, invented in 1884 by Ottmar Mergenthaler, was regarded as the greatest advance in printing since the development of movable type 400 years earlier. This invention, which helped revolutionize the printing industry as the first practical mechanized typecasting machine, produced solid lines of text cast from rows of matrices. Each matrix was a block of metal—usually brass—into which an impression of a letter had been engraved or stamped and then transferred mechanically to a mold-making device producing a bar of type. After its use for printing, metal was melted down for use again; this made it much faster than hand typesetting and required fewer employees. This typesetting machine provided a new freedom in the creation of printed materials from newspapers and books, to labels and other forms of packaging and became a popular tool for visual communication.

A lithographers directory in 1887 included Robert Gair, the pioneer of machine-made cartons, and George Harris & Sons, who printed colorful cigar boxes. Business listings used the titles "Label Manufacturers," "Labels-Cigar," and "Label for Druggists." Lithographed cigar labeling was a topic that even *The New York Sun* referred to in 1888, commenting that "a few years ago any kind of label was considered good enough to put on a cigar box. Then they cost about $10 for 1,000, the average price paid now is $50. The label is often better than the cigar."

Miniatuur Box
(above)

Gee Bees Tin
The decorative elements on these two packaging designs were clearly influenced by the styles of the times.

The New Economy

With the effects of the industrial revolution throughout Europe, the mid-1800s saw a large-scale shift from rural to urban life. There were massive changes in the nature of work, the growing consumer economy, women's roles in society, and even in the size and nature of families. Up until this time most products were essentially luxuries that served what was known as "the carriage trade" or upper-class customers. New machinery and technologies brought about new products and services that were available to the masses. Manufacturers traded nationally and internationally as railways and steamships made the movement of goods over long distances easier. The progress of packaging design grew with this new phenomenon: the national and international marketing and distribution of consumer goods.

New production and distribution methods of the late nineteenth century changed the way food was integrated with culture through packaging materials. Industrial plastics development started in the mid-1800s with celluloid material used for photographic film. In 1899 wax seal packaging, invented by Henry G. Eckstein, provided a new opportunity for manufacturers to distribute perishable goods and provide freshness. These advances in packaging technology made some traditional goods, including flour and meat, more widely available. The hermetically sealed containers, which offered consumers shelf-stable food products, were a major development in the history of food packaging. The use of tin cans to cook and seal food now helped provide a year-round food supply. All of the products that used theses new inventions were communicated through the packaging design. This was just the beginning of packaging design being revised to communicate technological innovations and product developments.

**Carnation
Condensed Milk**
Photo: Ian House,
The American Package Museum,
www.packagemuseum.com

The signature "Carnation" typography, the fleur di lis icon, the word usage of the term brand and the flowers are all elements that support the communication of a reliable, trustworthy, friendly product.

**Crown Closure
Patent Illustration**
(facing page)
www.uspto.gov

This patent illustration demonstrates that innovations in bottle sealing devices were developed as early as 1892.

W. PAINTER.
BOTTLE SEALING DEVICE.

No. 468,258.   Patented Feb. 2, 1892.

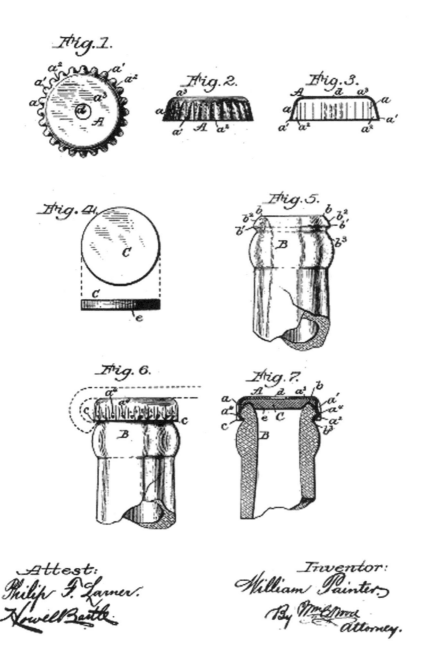

Attest:
Philip F. Larner.
Howell Beatll.

Inventor:
William Painter
By McElroy
Attorney.

Twentieth-Century Developments

With the assembly line instituted by Henry Ford in 1913, mass production took off in the United States. The government was struggling with how to manage a free market system and yet protect concerns of the consumer. The 1906 Federal Food and Drugs Act, which prohibited the use of false or misleading labeling, was one of the first regulations imposed on packaging design. This act did not require an accurate statement of ingredients or a correct statement of weight or measure, and the mandate to prevent misleading packaging was difficult to enforce. In 1913 the Gould Amendment required a statement of net quantity of contents of food. This amendment stated that the packaging was misbranded if the quantity of the contents could not be plainly marked on the outside of the package in terms of weight, measure, or numerical count. It was thought that this act did little to protect the consumer since many consumers didn't take notice of the weight statement and purchased the product based on size and shape. United States Supreme Court Justice Louis D. Brandeis described the principle of the time as "caveat emptor," or let the buyer beware. With the sale of inferior or impure goods making consumers wary, honest merchants marked their goods with their own identification, for consumer protection as well as to build awareness of their brand.

Nabisco Animal Crackers
In 1902 the National Biscuit Company introduced Barnum's Animals Crackers. The packaging design of a circus wagon had a string handle so the box could be hung as a Christmas ornament. This current packaging design remains relatively unchanged.

Clearly the mutual dependence of nineteenth-century products upon packaging materials and design cannot be overemphasized. In the consumer's mind the connection was being made—the product and the packaging were perceived as one and the same. Matches could not have been sold without a matchbox, dry goods were filled into boxes with proper and affordable methods of filling and storing products, and canned goods were providing safely preserved foods and consumer convenience.

Trademarked products became established, and brand names such as Heinz, Ivory, and Nestlé sought to make their products appealing to the public and through advertising made them known worldwide. Packaging designs of consumer products were illustrated for newspaper advertisements, catalogues, signs and posters. The growth of this form of pictorial advertising had a significant impact on the advancement of packaging design.

A large number of technical innovations led to the continued improvement of packaging and, consequently, to increased choice of food, thereby improving the everyday standard of living and increasing the demand on the design of the packaging. The use of aluminum foil, which was developed when the first aluminum plant opened in Switzerland in 1910, made it possible to effectively seal medications and other

HANDS that are admired for their whiteness and smoothness generally belong to the woman who knows the value of Ivory Soap for household purposes as well as for bath and toilet.

She washes dishes with Ivory Soap. She does most of her laundry work with it. And she uses it for much of her general cleaning.

In her housework, as in her personal toilet, Ivory Soap enables her to avoid continual contact with strong suds which redden and roughen the skin faster than lotions can restore its natural color and smoothness.

At the same time, the purity and quality of Ivory make it cleanse even more thoroughly than alkaline soap. And as to cost, it is priced so low that the actual outlay for household soap is practically no greater where Ivory Soap is used than if the work were done with ordinary laundry soap.

IVORY SOAP . . . . 99 44/100 % PURE

IT FLOATS

Factories at Ivorydale, Ohio ; Port Ivory, New York; Kansas City, Kansas; Hamilton, Canada

Heinz Fifty-Seven Varieties Advertisement
(above)

Ivory Soap Advertisement
(left)
The Ladies Home Journal, April 1915. Trademarked products became established, and brand names such as Heinz and Ivory sought to make their products appealing to the public and through advertising made them known worldwide.

air-sensitive products such as tobacco and chocolate. The invention of transparent cellophane in the early 1920s marked the beginning of the era of plastics. Every decade since has seen the introduction of new plastic materials. Today plastic, in all of its forms and formulas, is one of the most widely used materials for packaging and products alike.

THE ORIGIN OF "PLASTICS"

Small vases known as "plastics" were molded into the shapes of animal and human heads. The origin of the word comes from the Latin *Plasticus*, and the Greek *Plasitkos* meaning to form, to mold, or to shape matter. Petroleum-based plastics are a very large group of synthetic materials whose structures are based on the chemistry of carbon and are made of extremely long chains of carbon atoms or polymers. Natural polymers include tar, shellac, tortoiseshell, and animal horn, as well as tree saps that produce amber and latex. Processed with heat and pressure, these polymers were turned into useful articles like hair ornaments and jewelry. Natural polymers began to be chemically modified during the 1800s to produce many materials—the most famous was celluloid. The first synthetic polymer was Bakelite, produced in the early 1900s. (See Chapter 8: Structures and Materials in Packaging Design)

After several decades of urbanization and industrialization, post-World War I America was marked by an increase in availability of mass-produced merchandise. The 1920s brought a boom in advertising as companies responded to postwar consumerism. New products, introduced at an accelerated rate, created demand and forced leading manufacturers to invent new ways of selling them. Products needed to look good, distinguish themselves from one another, and reflect the ever-changing values of the consumer if they were to sell. The marketing of product became a priority, and the business of packaging design developed as an important strategy for consumer products companies.

CLARENCE BIRDSEYE: THE FATHER OF FROZEN FOOD

In 1920 Clarence Birdseye invented and later advanced a quick-freezing system, which enabled fresh food to be flash-frozen. The process safely preserved the taste and appearance of food as it was packed in waxed cartons. Although the practice of preserving food by freezing can be traced back to the early seventeenth century and the first business that produced frozen food took place in the late seventeenth century.

Birds Eye Foods
Photo: Birds Eye Foods, Inc.
Early packaging design.

The American middle class was a growing consumer base by the 1930s. Women began to play a greater role in the economy as the decision makers for most household purchases. Marketers competed for their attention and for ways to attract them to the marketplace. The invention of the first shopping cart, introduced in 1937 at Standard Food Stores, added significantly to the shopping experience. Consumers had to pick out their own purchases instead of requesting the items from a store clerk. The shopping cart provided consumers the convenience of not having to carry all their purchases. This tool helped to increase the numbers of purchases made at one time, which in turn thrilled the retailers. Women from all socioeconomic levels now did the

Birds Eye Foods First Advertisement
Photo: Birds Eye Foods, Inc.

The marketing of product through advertising was fairly commonplace. However, now the business of packaging design developed into a significant strategy for consumer products companies.

Early Supermarket
Shoppers relied
on the local grocer
to recommend
brands and even to
weight and package
products.

majority of shopping. They shopped often and prided themselves for their ability to discern reasonably priced goods. Packaging designs competed for their attention as the number of product choices grew in the marketplace. In the mid-1940s packaging was improved for frozen food. Vegetables and fish products, considered a luxury after the wartime rationing, were among the introductions in the frozen food category. Although aerosol cans (with a propellant system and a spray valve) had been invented as early as 1927, it was not until the spray valve was perfected in the 1940s that they became a significant packaging structure in the market. Tin, steel, and aluminum were the materials used to manufacture cans. The first heavy steel cans were replaced by aluminum and aerosol cans, which became an inexpensive way to dispense liquids, foams, powders, and creams. Beverage cans, first launched in the United States in the mid-1930s, were made in four parts with a crown cork closure (see Crown Closure Patent illustration, page 15).

The Growth of the Packaging Design Business

By the early 1930s packaging was blossoming into a mature industry. A variety of publications served suppliers, designers, and clients with the latest information in the field. *Advertising Age*, launched in 1930, devoted attention to packaging design, as did industry-specific magazines such as *American Druggist*, *Tea and Coffee Trade Journal*, and *Progressive Grocer*. The publication of magazines such as *Modern Packaging* in 1927 and *Packaging Record* in 1930 indicated the complexity of this growing profession and the collaboration of consumer product companies with packaging design and advertising leaders, packaging materials manufacturers, printers, and others in production roles.

Companies that manufactured and supplied packaging materials were a resource for packaging designers. These companies, as well as printing firms, often were called upon to provide technical and creative assistance and to supply sample materials.

Some large industrial corporations created package development departments such as DuPont in 1929, and the Container Corporation of America in 1935. Collaboration among the three sources for packaging design—the design firm, the in-house staff at manufacturing companies, and the employees at suppliers—persisted from that time on.

In the 1930s advertising agencies, such as NW Ayer, provided packaging design services. For some consumer product companies, such as Avon Products and Sears Roebuck, the demand for packaging design was significant enough to have a staff of design personnel. Other businesses hired industrial-design professionals as "consumer engineers" and "product stylists" that could apply their artistic abilities to create designs that would satisfy consumer demand. These new industrial designers were the professionals charged with creative leadership to support the modern consumer product industry. The leaders of modern packaging design were professionals from diverse backgrounds. Walter Dorwin Teague and John Vassos both began their careers in advertising; Donald Deskey, Norman Bel Geddes, Russell Wright, and Henry Dreyfuss started out designing sets for theaters; and French immigrant Raymond Loewy brought his European sensibility to the consumer arts. Edwin H. Sheele, Roy Sheldon, and Francesco Gianninoto, all industrial designers, were able to move seamlessly into both product and packaging design.

Understanding the technical factors of packaging design was an important issue for designers at this time, in order to avoid creating something that could not be produced or that would not work with current machinery or production lines. A broad understanding of packaging materials, manufacturing, printing, labeling, and shipping was essential for the success of the end result.

In Arthur Pulos's *The American Design Adventure 1940-1975*, the industrial designer Ben Nash is credited with "doing more than any other designer of his time to turn packaging design into a profession by fusing technological and merchandising practicalities with aesthetic and psychological values." By 1935 Nash's firm had more than 30 designers on staff in his New York office.

Modern Packaging
Cover, January 1936

These designers grasped the idea that working with the manufacturer at the beginning of the project rather than with the retailer at the end would prove most successful. They believed that a design assignment would be easier if there were known parameters: what was the product to do, how was it made, what materials were to be used, and where was it to be sold. This information guided the designers to create packages that provided a true reflection of the product without the use of deceptive styling. The concept of an agreed understanding of design constraints as a means to successfully guide a project is the framework of the creative methodology used today.

These early designers, with their diverse backgrounds, were the masters of a new profession of creating art for industry. Young designers came from commercial graphic design, theatrical set design, typography, fashion illustration, and engineering. Over time successful design professionals had developed a common set of principles to guide their business practices and processes.

Although aesthetic appearance was important, safety, convenience, cost of production, and choice of materials guided the creative process. It was determined early on that although appearance may lead a consumer to make a purchase, it could not lead to product satisfaction. The ideal product provided the perfect compliment of form and function.

Among one of the significant effects World War II had on packaging design was the explosion of the supermarket and prepackaged food. Where there was once a local store clerk to weigh and package the product, the container now existed independently in this new marketplace. This changed the marketplace forever as consumers came to rely less on their grocer to provide them with information about a product. Although in Europe many goods were still sold in bulk, new mass marketing in the United States caused goods to be sold in prepackaged form.

The growth of self-service stores in the late 1940s forced the need for packaging design to be quickly identifiable and was often termed "the silent salesman." However, without a salesman there was no one to plug a particular brand. Packaging design was propelled further into a dynamic profession devoted to making consumer products more enticing to the discriminating public and to making consumer brand recognition integral to product marketing. In this new competitive marketplace, packaging design was responsible for promoting a brand and positioning itself prominently on the retail shelf. Food manufacturers became food marketers, and brand management, product marketing, advertising, and packaging design consultancies grew enormously.

Consumer Protection

In 1962 President Kennedy addressed the U.S. Congress with the first presidential address devoted to consumer interest. In this speech he recognized that the consumers' rights to safety, information, choice, freshness, convenience, and attractiveness needed protection. Gaps between the existing regulatory bodies— the Food and Drug Administration (FDA), Federal Trade Commission (FTC), and U.S. Department of Agriculture (USDA)—meant that the consumer was inadequately protected. As a result of the work of consumer interest groups and Esther Peterson, the Special Assistant to the President on Consumer Affairs, Kennedy enacted the Fair Packaging and Labeling Act in 1967.

Birds Eye Frozen Foods Section
The growth of self-service stores in the late 1940s forced the need for packaging design to be quickly identifiable and was often termed "the silent salesman."

THE FAIR PACKAGING AND LABELING ACT

The Fair Packaging and Labeling Act (FPLA) directed the Federal Trade Commission and the Food and Drug Administration to issue regulations requiring that all "consumer commodities" be labeled to disclose net contents, identity of commodity, and name and place of business of the product's manufacturer, packer, or distributor. The act authorized additional regulations where necessary to prevent consumer deception (or to facilitate value comparisons) with respect to descriptions of ingredients, slack fill of packages, use of "cents-off" or lower price labeling, and characterization of package sizes. The Office of Weights and Measures of the National Institute of Standards and Technology, U.S. Department of Commerce, was authorized to promote to the uniformity in state and federal regulations of the labeling of consumer commodities.

The enactment of the Fair Packaging and Labeling Act of 1967 now federally mandated label and packaging accuracy. As a result consumer product companies needed to revise their packaging to meet these new standards. With this new demand, design firms expanded their capabilities to include packaging design. Henry J. Stern, First Deputy Commissioner, Department of Consumer Affairs, the City of New York, commented, "The future of packaging depends, in great part, on the industry's understanding of consumer demands. The public is learning that packages often fail to supply factual information about the products, and they are not satisfied. Retail buyers, not manufacturers, are the ultimate consumers of the packaging industry. They want packages to disclose, not conceal and inform, not deceive. Industry must meet these standards on its own initiatives. If it fails, the consequences will be more government regulation."

Screaming Yellow Zonkers
Packaging design influenced by the 1960s typographic styles of Lubalin and Glaser.

Advancements in Packaging Design

The scientific and technical accomplishments of NASA (National Aeronautics Space Administration) did much to advance packaging materials and technology. Bite-size cubes, freeze-dried powders, squeezable aluminum tubes, and beverage packaging made from a foil laminate were all developed to provide protection, convenience, accessibility, and longer shelf life.

The advancements in typography in the 1960s supported the need for packaging design to communicate the visual personality of the product more immediately. With phototypesetting (the direct image of the text obtained in either positive or negative, according to need, on a photosensitive, usually transparent surface by exposing the surface to light through transparent matrices, negative or positive, of the letters and symbols) designers had greater control over letter spacing and line spacing. With the commercial typographic work of designers such as Herb Lubalin and Milton Glaser, typographic mastery grew as a highly valued art form.

Typography, graphic design, packaging design, and advertising, deemed commercial art, was clearly part of the cultural landscape in the later part of the twentieth century, and was challenged by the Pop Art movement in redefining the boundaries between fine and commercial art. Pop Art celebrated postwar consumerism and bridged the gap between what was "high art" and "low art" by using common, everyday mass-produced objects and making them appear grand and unique. Andy Warhol's screened prints of Coca-Cola bottles, Brillo boxes, and Campbell's soup cans elevated packaging design to Pop Art status and forever embossed these images in our American cultural iconography.

During the 1960s, increased competition created the need for corporations to reflect a unified and consistent image to the public as a means of strong identification. Graphic materials that represented the company's public image—such as letterheads, logotypes, truck signage, and business cards—became part of a company's "corporate identity." The emphasis on corporate identity and the outpouring of new products during this period forced companies to update and unify their product's visual image regularly to create a stronger and more lasting impression of the company in the minds of the consumers.

Marketers now saw most products as having established affinities that reflected gender roles, class, race, and other social characteristics of consumers. In a 1960 publication titled "Package Research...An Aid to Design," author Edward W. J. Fasion commented that fancy beer labels, which appeal to all the marketing people, do not appeal to most "heavy beer drinkers," who as blue-collar workers had different tastes and therefore reacted negatively to delicately scroll styled labels, which were more appropriate for women. Marketers realized that different brands appealed to different kinds of people and that brand image is what sells the product.

The need for distinctive sales packaging forced manufacturers to develop new materials and structures. Packaging designers needed to adapt existing designs not only to new packaging forms but to meet federally mandated requirements.

Through the mid-1960s the economy in the United States grew more quickly than ever. Production exceeded consumer demand,

"The Souper Dress" 1966–67
Photo: Irving Solero, courtesy of the Museum at the Fashion Institute of Technology, New York.
Museum Purchase P90.87.1
The Museum at FIT

Pattern of Campbell's Soup cans on nonwoven "paper" dress—the impact of Andy Warhol's art elevated packaging design to pop art status.

Beer Cans
The delicately scroll styled labels did not appeal to most "heavy beer drinkers."

so competition increased. New products entered the market at a rapid rate, and product failures were up as profits were down. Increasingly, sophisticated consumers were harder to reach; they showed greater shopping selectivity, were suspicious of false claims, and appeared totally unimpressed with superficial product or packaging changes.

As product differences were becoming almost negligible or completely nonexistent, manufacturers began to look for methods to distinguish their products from the competition. While changes happened in the distribution and selling of goods, technological breakthroughs advanced new production techniques, processes, and entirely new material concepts, including new plastics. Many industry leaders, faced with the challenges presented by marketing and technology, initiated an ambitious new product development period.

In 1966 designer Alan Berni urged manufacturers to concentrate on the development of metal surfaces to provide the designer with greater creative flexibility in creating unique packaging. Other designers, including Hayward Blake, suggested that more attention be directed to the "tactile aspect" of the container design. Among the developments of the time was grainless paperboard that allowed designers to develop contour-shaped and multicurved packages.

By the 1970s a number of packaging design firms had offices internationally. Raymond Loewy's offices had worked on the packaging designs of Maxwell House, Kellogg's, Nabisco, Quaker Oats, Ivory, Duncan Hines, Heinz, and Betty Crocker. The role of packaging design had become one of expressing a well-defined marketing strategy—more than a container and point-of-sale billboard than considered previously.

L'Eggs Egg Packaging Design
Client: Sara Lee Corporation
Design Firm: Howard Marlboro Group
Designer: Paul Fulton and HMG

The L'Eggs eggs literally cracked open the consumer's awareness of the power of packaging design.

1970s Coffee Competition
Packaging design began to take on such strong marketing positions that it became nearly indiscernible from the product itself.

1970s Pierre Cardin Fragrance
The structure of this suggestive packaging design epitomized the decade.

THE ADVENT OF APPLE

The year 1977 marked the incorporation of Apple Computer, with Steve Jobs at the helm and the launch of the Apple II personal computer. The Apple Macintosh platform, which began with Macintosh 128K, changed the design world forever and established Apple computer technology as the cornerstone of any design business today.

Apple established itself as a design leader with the launch of the first iMac computers in an assortment of "flavors"—bright colors radically different from the standard beige color of computers and other hardware devices. The iMac flavors started a trend not only in the computer industry but also in other categories, including small electronics, office supplies, housewares, and fashion accessories.

By the 1980s the growth of large shopping centers and supermarkets spurred the demand for more products. Supermarkets expanded their food operations, offering all types of prepared take-home foods. Small specialty shops within the market brought back the nostalgia of the local butcher, florist, and baker, prompting a new direction for packaging designs and a greater demand for merchandising display systems. During this period of intense competition, the products sold in supermarkets depended even more heavily on their packaging design for their success. Due to the steady increase in marketplace competition and the realization by both marketers and manufacturers that good design is a corporate asset, there was a significant growth of the number of design firms throughout the country. New firms were established and existing firms opened offices in other regions of the country to meet the assignments of redesigning stagnant brands, extending the lines of existing brands, and designing new brands. Packaging design gained worldwide recognition.

**Quaker Oats
Life Cereal**
With an advertising campaign of "Let's get Mikey to try it" Quaker Oats recognized the power of placing him directly onto the package.

Celentano Frozen Foods
The use of appetite appeal and the simplicity of a clean white packaging design created immediate brand recognition for Celentano.

During the 1980s design associations that supported the interests of packaging designers expanded their goals of networking, creating public awareness of the profession, and enhancing communication among design professionals. Membership in organizations such as the Package Design Council (United States), The Design Council (United Kingdom), the Japan Package Design Association, the Thai Packaging Association, and the World Packaging Association gained recognition both nationally and internationally. In the United States, The Coleman Group, Deskey Associates, Gerstman + Meyers, Landor Associates, Mittleman and Robinson, Primo Angeli, the Schecter Group, and Teague Associates were among the numerous design firms whose primary business was devoted to packaging design.

Ending a Century

By the 1990s manufacturers, with their many products branded and merchandised together, recognized the need to make packaging engineers part of the product development team and packaging designers part of the marketing team. The demand for convenience and value dictated many aspects of material development and marketing. Space efficiency, reusability, and environmental concerns also gained in importance as a reflection of the changing values of consumer society. Soda cans shifted from pull tabs to easy-to-open tops, glass was replaced by plastic to support consumer concerns about breakage, and laminates and specialty coatings on paperboard all provided new design opportunities for packaging designers.

A 1998 *Fast Company* magazine article by Daniel Pink about Harvard professor Jerry Zaltman stated that the average American supermarket had approximately 30,000

Starbucks Coffee Packaging
(above left)
Client: Starbucks Coffee Company
Design Firm: Hornall Anderson Design Works
Designers: Jack Anderson, Julie Lock, Mary Hermes, Julia LaPine, David Bates, Denise Weir, John Anicker, Lian Ng

Evian Millennium Bottle
(above)
The proprietary teardrop-shaped bottle of Evian introduced the new millennium.

SKUs (Stock Keeping Unit: a specific product's numeric identifier represented in a scannable bar code as a means of keeping inventory of a product), approximately 50 percent more than five years earlier. With mergers between consumer product companies and innovations in technology, products began seeing even shorter life cycles.

Opportunities for packaging designers skyrocketed as companies sought to redesign their packages to provide more immediate communication. The product's message, conveyed through the design, must now grab the consumers' attention and make the sale in a shorter time period than ever before.

Design Today

With luxury being among the top values of consumers in the early twenty-first century, design has moved to the forefront as the means of differentiating high quality. Design—from that of fashion, home products, and automotive to cell phones and computers—has become the critical factor in a world of consumerism. With the consumers' aesthetic sensibilities sharpened by the quality of design, they are more keenly aware of the power packaging design its impact on purchasing decisions.

Packaging designs today have many varied objectives. Although there is no one theme or approach that can tie together the state of packaging design in the early twenty-first century, "simplicity" seems to be an emerging philosophy.

SIMPLICITY

In an article "Be Smart, Be Simple" by Rob Wallace, of Wallace Church, stated, "Simplicity is the most effective design and communications aesthetic. New visual strategies are connecting brands to consumers at a visceral level via stripped-down brand identities and communications. The most successful brands are able to connect with their core enthusiasts using an effective 'visual shorthand.'" He continues, "Using color, symbols, icons, and a singularity of focus, [these] brands cut through the visual noise. The key strategy shared by these new successful brands is that their messages, their identities, and their entire communications architectures are, quite simply, simple."

Packaging design today is fully integrated into a company's all-encompassing brand strategy. With their long history of administering brands, packaging designers are critical to the partnership of business and are required to have an understanding not only of visual communication and structural design but of marketing, finance, sociology, psychology, economics, and international trade.

The examination of packaging design throughout history begins with the needs of people. Throughout our changing societies, competition in the marketplace, historical events, shifting lifestyles, and advancements through discoveries and inventions, no one single cause has influenced the development of packaging design. Multiple factors continue to impact the discipline and the profession's forward development

2 DEFINING PACKAGING DESIGN

Packaging Design as Communication

Packaging design is a creative business that connects form, structure, materials, color, imagery, typography, and ancillary design elements with product information to make a product suitable for marketing. Packaging design serves to contain, protect, transport, dispense, store, identify, and distinguish a product in the marketplace. Ultimately packaging design resolves the marketing objectives of the product by distinctively communicating a consumer product's personality or function.

Through a comprehensive design methodology, packaging design uses many tools to solve complex marketing problems. Brainstorming, exploration, experimentation, and strategic thinking are some of the fundamental ways that visual and verbal information is shaped into a concept, idea, or design strategy. Through an effectively resolved design strategy product information is communicated to the consumer.

Packaging design must function as the aesthetic means of communicating to people from all different backgrounds, interests, and experiences, therefore, an awareness of anthropology, sociology, psychology, ethnography, and linguistics can benefit the design process and the appropriate design choices. Specifically an understanding of social and cultural variations, nonbiological human behaviors, and cultural preferences and distinctions can aid in the comprehension of how visual elements communicate.

An understanding of psychology and the study of mental processes and behaviors can assist in analyzing human motivation through visual perception. Knowledge of basic linguistics—including phonetics (speech sounds, spelling), semantics (meaning), and syntax (arrangement)—can help in the proper usage and application of language. In addition, mathematics, architecture, material sciences, business, and international trade are areas that directly relate to packaging design.

Visual problem solving is at the core of packaging design. Whether it is introducing a new product or improving the appearance of an existing one, creative skills—from conceptualizing and rendering to three-dimensional design, design analysis, and technical problem solving—are the ways a design problem is resolved into innovative solutions. The goal is not to create designs that are purely visually appealing since packaging designs that are solely aesthetically pleasing do not necessarily achieve marketable results. Creatively accomplishing the marketer's strategic objective through an appropriate design solution is the primary function of packaging design.

As a creative tool, packaging design is a means of expression. It cannot be overstated that this is product expression, not personal expression, and that the designer or marketer's own personal bias—whether it be color, shape, material, or typographic style—should have little bearing on a packaging design. A product's expression, one that attracts a target consumer market, is achieved through a creative process in which physical and visual elements work together to communicate emotional, cultural, social, psychological, and informational cues to the target consumer.

Packaging Design Paradigms
A design concept has to perform on many aesthetic and functional levels.

Egg and Egg Carton
The shell of an egg is a perfect package, but the egg carton is the packaging.

PACKAGING AND A PACKAGE

Packaging refers to the act of wrapping or covering an item or group of items. Cellophane, paper, textile, glass, plastic, fabric, and metal are among the hundreds of materials used for the purpose of packaging. A box, can, wrapper, carton, bag, jar, and tube are among the hundreds of packaging forms.

A *package*, on the other hand, refers to the physical object itself—the carton, container, or bundle. A package can be a pack of cigarettes or a parcel from the post office. This broad indeterminate term is all too often used in an all-encompassing manner. The expression "the package" implies the final result of the process of packaging. This generic reference does little to distinguish this dynamic design medium or its planned function—to contain, transport, dispense, and so on. *Package* is a noun—it is an object. *Packaging* is a verb, reflecting the ever-changing nature of the medium.

Packaging Design in the Marketing Mix

Marketing is defined as planning and executing the conception and development, pricing, placement, promotion, and distribution of ideas, goods, and services to create exchanges that satisfy individual and organizational objectives. As a business activity involved in the moving of goods from the producer to the consumer, marketing includes advertising and packaging design, merchandising and sales.

As a material component of a society, products foster economic growth and satisfy the human need to employ our physical resources. With the continuous burgeoning of consumerism comes the proliferation of products and services. In the average supermarket there are tens of thousands of different products that line the shelves. Department stores, mass merchandisers, specialty stores, outlets, and the Internet are all retail opportunities and in these environments products are brought to life by their packaging design. In fact, products have become so inescapably intertwined in all aspects our life that they are no longer objects of necessity but of desire.

With the vastness of consumer choice comes product competition. Competition in turn fosters the need for market distinction and differentiation. Packaging design serves to visually communicate product differentiation. Think about it from an appearance standpoint, without distinctive packaging design for all the brands of various products-including bread, milk, and vegetables to perfume, lipstick, and liquor—each product would look remarkably similar.

Comparable Products
Products in the same category and in the same structure would appear identical if not for their packaging design.

Marketers are ultimately responsible for determining their product's distinguishing characteristics and providing a clear contrast between products. The difference may be in ingredients, performance, manufacturing or there may not be any discernible difference between similar products. Marketing is often simply about creating the perception of a difference. Whatever it is, the marketer defines the approach that would capitalize on what makes their products salable and the race begins for product differentiation.

Ideally, when the packaging design provides the consumer with clear and specific information (whether consciously or subconsciously), and possibly a point of comparison (which one appears to be a more effective product, a better value, a more convenient package), a purchase is incited. Whether it's a calculated decision or an impulse buy, the physical look of the product's packaging is frequently the sole reason for a product's sale. These ultimate goals—to stand out among competitors, to avoid consumer confusion, and to influence the consumer in a purchasing decision—make packaging design a critical factor in the success of a company's integrated brand marketing plan.

Reaching the Target Market

The role of packaging design as a selling tool is most effective when a marketer has identified a niche to claim or a specific consumer group to target. Though companies want to sell the most products to the largest number of consumers, defining an

Dirty Girl
Client: Blue Q
Design Firm: Haley Johnson Design
Designer: Haley Johnson
Art Director: Mitch Nash

The niche marketing of the Dirty Girl line of products uses a novel design approach to attract young consumers.

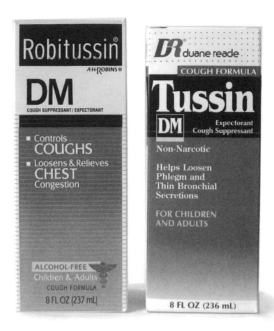

audience provides a clear focus for the marketing of the product and its packaging design. A clearly defined "target market"—one in which consumers' values, preferences, lifestyles, and habits are circumscribed—provides a framework that helps determine design strategies and appropriate product communications.

Other considerations include the determination of which consumer base would benefit most from the product or who would be most accessible and receptive to the product. Marketing would use this as a means of directing packaging design and advertising to attract this target consumer group.

In the competitive retail arena the packaging design must visually attract, stimulate interest and awareness, and affect a consumer's purchasing decision—in the blink of an eye. Therefore, the goal is to have unique features that distinguish it as the product of a specific brand or manufacturer. For many brands, the packaging design establishes the visual look of the category, and competitors compete by adopting a similar appearance. Uses of color, typographic styles, characters, structure, and other design elements become category cues for consumers.

Proprietary Features

Typographic style, graphic imagery, and color can be considered proprietary or "ownable" elements of a packaging design if they are customized and possess a distinctive feature. Often a proprietary attribute can be protected legally by trademark or registration with the government. (See Chapter 12: Understanding Legal Issues) With extended use in commerce over time, these unique features are connected

Robitussin DM vs. Duane Reade Tussin DM
Certain store brands or private-label products are intentionally designed to look similar to the leading brands.

**Proprietary
Water Bottle**
Proprietary structural design has become an essential component in the proliferation of new product entries in the beverage categories. An exclusive structural design form or feature helps differentiate in the myriad competition and also speaks to consumer needs and wants of portability and convenience.

with the brand in the eyes of the consumer. Designed with the intent to convey the characteristics "unique" and "ownable," proprietary packaging design can be a means toward this end.

Packaging Design and the Brand

If packaging design is part of the bigger picture of what is termed *brand*, then what defines a brand? In its most basic form brand is the trade name given to a product or service. In today's world, however, the term brand has become all-encompassing. Although it is a term that has been used for decades, it is overused, and defined in many ways by various professions. From the perspective of packaging design, a brand is a name, a mark of ownership and the representation of products, services, people, and places. This includes everything from stationery and printed materials, product names, packaging design, advertising design, signage, uniforms, and even architecture.

Brands are defined by their presence in our consumer society, by their products' physical attributes and emotional connotations, and by how they relate to consumers' aspirations. The brand becomes the means by which a company differentiates itself in the minds of consumers.

XanGo Beverage
Client: XanGo, LLC
Design Firm: Flowdesign
Designer: Dan Matauch

The new XanGo brand is the "category-creator" of a mangosteen fruit drink and dietary supplement high in anti-oxidant benefits. The proprietary bottle design and brand identity was created to "capture the essence of XanGo and its Thailand origins with a mix of contemporary and traditional shapes, colors, and icons," says Dan Matauch, Flowdesign's principal and creative director.

Brand Evolution

One way to look at brands is as if they were human. Brands are conceived of and then they are born, they grow, and they continue to evolve. They have identifiable characteristics that distinguish themselves from others. Their designs define themselves and communicate their purpose and position. In fact, the term *evolutionary* is commonly used in packaging design to refer to the process by which brands grow and develop over time. An evolutionary change refers to minor design changes that happen in the brand, while revolutionary refers to radical changes.

In *The Brand Gap*, Marty Neumeier states, "A brand is a person's gut feeling about a product, service, or company. It's a gut feeling because we're all emotional, intuitive beings, despite our best efforts to be rational. It's a person's gut feeling because in the end the brand is defined by individuals, not by companies, markets, or the so-called general public."

For many consumers there is little distinction between the brand and the packaging design. Through the combination of three-dimensional materials and structure with two-dimensional visual communication elements, packaging design creates the image of the brand and builds the relationship between the consumer and the product. The packaging design visually articulates the brand's promise, whether it is quality, value, performance, safety, or convenience.

Brand Identity

The brand identity is the tangible aspect of the brand—the essential components including the name, color, symbol, and other design elements. The visual representation of these elements and their combination defines the brand and differentiates the products and/or services of one marketer from another. The brand identity creates an emotional connection with the consumer. Whether it conveys abstract or concrete ideas about a product, when fused in the mind of the consumer the identity becomes the mental picture or perception of the product. A brand connection is a "must-have" for marketing success.

Brand Promise

Brand promise is the assurance or guarantee by the marketer or manufacturer about the product and its claims. In packaging design the brand promise is communicated through the brand identity. Fulfillment of a brand's promise is key to gaining consumer loyalty and assuring a product's success on the shelf.

Brand promise can be broken, as can any other promise, when it is not kept. There are many different ways this can occur and when it happens not only is the reputation of the brand and the manufacturer discredited, but consumers may choose to go elsewhere.

The brand promise and perceived value of a product can be adversely affected due to the following failures of its packaging design:

- The design fails to function properly by not dispensing or opening easily.
- The typographic application is difficult to read and the product name is hard to pronounce or understand. For example, the text on the packaging design is illegible or poorly communicates the product's function.
- The design communicates a product superior to its competition, but the product is inferior. For example, the appetizing photograph does not resemble the actual appearance of the contents.

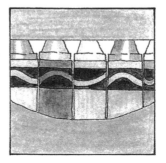

Brand Identity Recall

Designer: Mayuko Hari/FIT (Fashion Institute of Technology)

Student sketches show how easily elements of a brand identity can be recalled.

- An overly elaborate design is perceived as too expensive so the consumer chooses not to buy the product. For example, the use of new papers, unnecessary die cuts, foil stamping, or other embellishments that try to impress but are perceived as frivolity.

- A poor-quality design is perceived as a cheaper product with inferior quality. For example, the packaging design's materials inappropriately reflect the quality, price point, and personality of the product.

- A design appears too similar to its competition and causes confusion in the market.

- The product contents are inaccurately reported on the packaging (e.g. net weight).

- The brand identity elements are out of scale with the packaging structure.

- Inconsistent, unbelievable, or inaccurate claims or images are included on the packaging.

- The packaging structure is difficult to use or unable to be scanned.

Brand Equity

As the packaging design becomes the image of the brand, consumers come to recognize and visually identify with the values, qualities, features, and attributes of the brand. From a marketing standpoint, the associations of the packaging design with the product—from the tangible physical structure and visual identity to the intangible emotional connection—become inextricably linked to the legitimacy and reliability of the brand. They can be measured by how much and how often the consumer identifies with them and become valuable assets or equities of the brand.

Companies manage their brand equities with utmost care. Since it is often difficult to separate the consumer's perception of the brand from the packaging, the elements that comprise the brand's identity are priceless. When a brand delivers on its commitment to product attributes and the promise of quality and value, it builds brand equity.

Brands become established category leaders because of the strength of their equities through the consistent delivery of their brand promise—a trustworthy, reliable, quality product. Consumers favor brands with strong reputations, which facilitates and simplifies product choice. Consumers will buy what they trust.

For existing brands, typography, symbols, icons, characters, colors, and structures are among the visual elements of a packaging design that can comprise a company's brand equity. For new brands that have a short history in the marketplace, there is no existing equity to build on. The packaging design establishes the new product's image in the eyes of the consumer.

Brand Loyalty

The notion of brand has everything to do with trust. Trust is built in the minds of consumers after having a good experience with the products that live under a brand name. If the experience is favorable, then a repeat purchase is made with the assumption that the experience will be the same. Brands thrive when they live up to their promise in the eyes of the consumer; the consumer continues to make repeat purchases, developing a preference for the brand. This preference establishes brand loyalty and is the producers' ultimate goal. When a consumer is devoted to a particular brand, they will take the time to seek it out and may even pay a higher price because of their firm belief in it. Strength and consistency are among the values that are integral components to brand loyalty. Loyal consumers believe in their brands in an almost fanatical way. Consider the brands consumers connect to and define themselves by— whether it's a handbag, a pair of jeans or shoes, or a car, brand loyalty is a means of personal identification.

Charmin "Call of Nature" Packaging
Client:
Procter & Gamble
Design Firm:
Interbrand
Designers:
Michael Endy,
Rick Murphy

Consumers have come to trust the Charmin brand for more than 75 years. The Charmin Bear has become part of the brand's equity since its introduction in 2000.

Brand Repositioning

Brand repositioning occurs when a company redefines a product's marketing strategy to compete more effectively and set the brand apart. In a repositioning, the visual brand equities of the current packaging design are assessed, design strategies and competitive opportunities are defined, and then a redesign process occurs. A new strategic direction for an existing packaging design emerges from this process. The goal of repositioning is to elevate the status of the brand and rival the competition within the marketplace.

The following are questions that begin the repositioning process:

- Are there strengths in the current packaging design?
- Does the consumer perceive visual identifiers or "cues" on the current packaging design?
- Does the packaging design have "ownable" qualities that enable the brand to stand apart from the competition?
- Does the packaging design differentiate itself from the competition effectively?

The answer of "yes" to the first three questions means that the packaging design has brand equities or visual elements that must be given careful consideration in the repositioning process. The aim in repositioning is to gain market share without losing brand equity.

Brand Extension

For the extension of a brand into new product lines, existing brand equities must be taken into consideration along with new marketing objectives. Existing design elements may be kept to maintain the consumer's perception of the brand promise.

A brand extension can be the introduction of new products in the same product category or a bold departure for the brand into a totally different category. Dependent on the product, the extension can introduce different varieties, flavors, ingredients, styles, sizes, and forms. In some cases it can be a new packaging design structure or evolutionary or revolutionary changes to the brand identity.

A prime example of brand extension is in the personal care (face, body, and hair) category. In any given brand there are can be myriad products, whether for specific treatments or for specific skin or hair types. Product-line offerings give consumers a greater variety of choices from the same manufacturer.

The product choice within a line extension can strengthen the manufacturer's brand in a variety of ways:

- When a product-line extension is positioned side by side on the shelf, the brand is strengthened by its shelf presence. The "wall" of products in a line creates a graphic billboard within the competitive shelf space.

- A brand of products presented in a group gives the consumer the sense that the marketer has vested in the quality and reliability of their products.

- If a consumer is satisfied with a brand and has choices within the categories in which the brand is positioned, he or she will be more loyal. Through the consumer's long-term investment brand equity is built.

Effective brands often establish the visual look of the packaging design within their category by adapting a similar appearance to their competitors. Color, typographic styles, use of characters, structure, and other design elements become category cues for consumers.

Skippy
Before redesign
(above left)
Client: Unilever
Design Firm:
Smith Design
Designer:
Laura Markley

The Skippy brand identity and packaging graphics had not been updated in many years. Building on existing equities, the Skippy logotype remains in red and still uses rounded letterforms, yet the logotype is updated—modified for a fun, bouncy appeal; the solution includes a brand character in the corner of each label.

Tahitian Noni
Original Packaging
Design, 2004

**Tahitian Noni
TePoema**
Line Extension, 2005
Client: Tahitian Noni
Design Firm:
Hornall Anderson
Design Works
Designers:
Jack Anderson,
Lisa Cervany,
James Tee,
Tiffany Place,
Leo Raymundo,
Jana Nishi,
Elmer dela Cruz,
Bruce Branson-
Meyer

**Coca-Cola and
Pepsi-Cola Bottles**
(facing page)
These two cola
brands, with very
similar-looking
logos in their early
brand history, have
dominated the
carbonated beverage
category for more
than a century.

Packaging Design and Society

As a part of the material ephemera of society, packaging design reveals much about the cultural values of the market. Since packaging designs exist primarily in marketplaces (the supermarket, mass merchandiser outlet, or department store), where people with varied cultural backgrounds and values come together, they must grab the consumer's attention immediately. This is achieved by employing the visuals and design elements that attract the target consumer. Through extensive market research and the planned employment of design elements, cultural symbols serve to communicate cultural values. Truly effective packaging design makes the consumer "see" themselves and their desires through the design elements on the packaging.

The impact of cultural values and beliefs on the purchasing decisions of the consumer cannot be overestimated. Fads, trends, health, fashion, art, age, upward mobility, and ethnicity are all revealed in the packaging designs in our marketplaces. In many cases the specific goal of the packaging design is to project these cultural values; in others the design communicates to the values of a broader consumer audience. In some instances the brand or the packaging design takes on a perceived value predicated on a very specific consumer population.

Packaging Design Objectives

Packaging design objectives are framed around the relevant marketing background and strategic objectives for a brand. Ideally the marketer or manufacturer provides specific, detailed information and points exactly to measurable goals for the packaging design. Answers to questions such as the following provide information that supports the packaging design process and provides a framework for the product's positioning in the marketplace:

- Who is the consumer?
- What environment will the product compete in?
- What price point will the product be set at?
- What are the production costs?
- What is the time frame from design to market?
- What distribution methods are planned?

Market positioning dictates placement of the product in the competitive retail environment and provides the basic foundation for the design direction. The packaging design's objectives become clearer once the marketing parameters are defined. The packaging design methodology, or the "how-to" process, is dictated by whether the objectives are to encompass the development of new products, the extension of existing brands into new product lines, or the repositioning of brands, products, or services.

Whether the packaging design is for a new or existing product, the primary objective of promoting sales is achieved through the quick and clear communication of the brand (brand promise) and the nature of the product (product attributes). Marketing research claims that 80 percent of all products that are touched by a consumer on the shelf are purchased. Breaking through the visual clutter of the competition is key.

Key points:

- Category Appropriateness
- Customization
- Consumer Experience
- Functionality

- Aesthetic Appeal
- Consumer Appeal
- Innovation
- Proprietary

Kit Kat Candy Bar
A report in the August 2005 BBC
News World Edition cited a surge
in the sales of Nestlé's Kit Kat bar in
Japan because the candy bar's name
is similar to the Japanese expression
kitto katsu, meaning good luck.
Parents and students alike purchased
them for "lucky charms" on exam days.

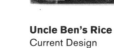

Uncle Ben's Rice
Package Design Magazine, March/April 1970
The brand identity for Uncle Ben's Rice reflects
the changing values of society.

Uncle Ben's Rice
Current Design

An excellent example of customization is the Jones Soda® brand. Its soul lies in the personalized, capricious imagery used for different flavors. By allowing consumers to submit their own photographs to be used on labels, the packaging design of this brand literally reflects the individuality of its products and its consumers. This fresh design approach breaks apart the consumers' preconceived notion of a national beverage brand and hits the mark in projecting a unique and customized brand personality that's always about the consumer.

POM Wonderful's eye-catching shape, first introduced in glass and now in plastic, makes a case for proprietary packaging structure because it clearly stands out in a crowded beverage category. The bulbous shape immediately communicates the essence of the brand based on its ingredient, the pomegranate.

Typically, packaging design objectives are specific to the particular product or brand. The packaging design may be directed to:

- Feature the unique attributes of the product;
- Strengthen the aesthetic appeal and the value of the product;
- Maintain uniformity within the brand's family of products;
- Strengthen differentiation between product varieties and lines;
- Develop distinctive packaging forms that are category-appropriate;
- Use new materials and develop innovative structures to reduce costs, be more environmentally friendly, or increase functionality.

Customized Jones Soda Labels
(below left)

POM Wonderful Bottles
(below)

Ideally a packaging design is evaluated regularly to ensure that it meets ever-changing marketing demands. Although it is difficult to apply metrics, rubrics, or other quantitative measurement tools to accurately determine the value of a specific packaging design, marketers review sales figures, collect data from consumer research, and conduct comparative analysis. These tools help determine the effectiveness of the packaging design in meeting the marketing objectives. In the end though, it is unreliable to place the financial success or failure of a product solely on its packaging design. Many variables affect consumers' buying behavior.

Ultimately, product developers, product manufacturers, packaging materials manufacturers, packaging engineers, marketers, and packaging designers all play a role in the success or failure of the packaging design in meeting the marketing objectives of a consumer brand.

Factors That Affect Packaging Design

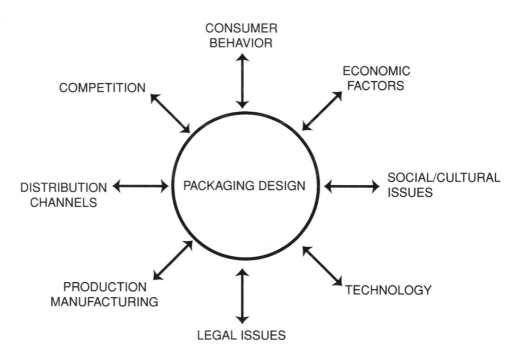

Packaging design fosters marketing success when:

- It reflects high quality at a fair market price.
- The product contents and marketer's message are clearly and immediately conveyed.
- It is durable and able to withstand shelf life and product use.
- Its elements are organized and efficacious, and do not appear soiled or adulterated on the shelf.
- It is category-appropriate.
- It is innovative and competitive.

Packaging design is influenced by:

- Consumer Behavior
- Sales Volume
- Market Share
- Market Growth
- Packaging (materials, sizes, proprietary design)
- Advertising/Marketing/Distribution
- Regional Trends
- Leading Brands/Competitors
- Retail Design
- Visual Merchandising/Display
- Point of Sale
- Demographics
- Projections

Packaging design is a result of:

- Research and Development
- Packaging Engineering
- Manufacturing
- Operations
- Sales
- Retail Buyers
- Advertising
- Promotions
- Purchasing
- Suppliers
- Designers
- Consumers

3 THE STAKEHOLDERS

The Stakeholders in Packaging Design

The packaging design business encompasses a wide range of industries and professions that serve to support the goals of marketing a consumer product. Each business has a specific role in the development of the consumer product, and many talented professionals directly impact the success of the end results. These are the professional stakeholders in the packaging design industry.

Traditionally the role of the stakeholders had been clearly defined. The marketer was in the advantageous position of decision maker while other industry professionals served as service providers or "vendors." However, with the advancement of technology, the evolved consumer design-consciousness, and the greater demands of retailing, marketers and the global business world no longer perceive the role of design as a means to an end but as a core component of a comprehensive corporate strategy.

With this new understanding of the value of design, marketers have come to rely heavily on the innovations, insights, and creative strategies of designers and suppliers in meeting their business objectives. Their knowledge, expertise, and ability to apply their creative and intuitive skills have made packaging design not only a highly respected business but one in which collaborative efforts are critical to marketing success.

The stakeholders that provide specific packaging design services are within the client-service relationship.

The creative service business stakeholders include:

- Design
- Illustration
- Industrial Design/Engineering
- Photography
- Production Management
- Printing
- Technology and Materials Supply

The consumer product business stakeholders include:

- Account Management
- Manufacturing
- Marketing/Brand Management
- Operations
- Product Development
- Production
- Promotion
- Purchasing
- Research
- Sales

INVOLVE THE STAKEHOLDERS

Beginning any packaging design assignment with the involvement of all the stakeholders saves time and money. Daniel A. Abramowicz, Ph.D., Executive VP Technology and Regulatory Affairs, Crown Holdings, Inc. states:

"For a product and its package to be successful it must satisfy a consumer's need on multiple levels. Gone are the days when we could afford to iterate several concepts in the marketplace. It is critical to ensure that the right concepts are being pursued every time. This can be done best by integrating the product development cycle with our customers' marketing departments, with design firms to ensure the aesthetics and package functionality are appropriate, and with consumer focus research to ensure the critical user interface is effective. We all have experienced the waste of time and money when such integration did not occur until very late in the concept development. Our customers need faster time to market with the highest opportunity for success, and such integration is critical to achieving that goal."

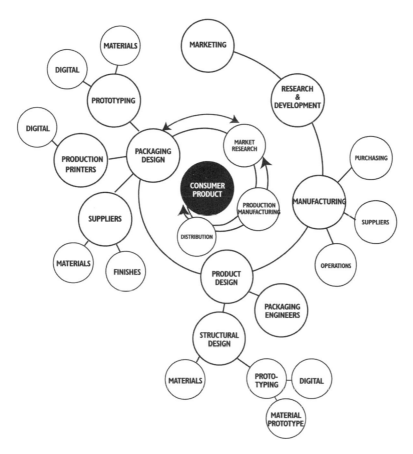

Professional Roles

Creative service professionals can work in-house within large or small consumer product corporations, for brand or packaging design firms, or as sole practitioners. Packaging design assignments involve teams of professionals or only the designer, client, and printer. A large design account may be handled by a small design firm and a small design account may be handled by a global design consultancy. Packaging designers collaborate with illustrators, photographers, industrial designers, production managers, material suppliers, and printers to serve the needs of the consumer products client.

The structure of both in-house design groups and design firms varies. The size of the business can dictate the composition of the organization and the organizational philosophy may establish the professional hierarchy. A small or large consumer products company can have one individual responsible for the packaging design, have a design team or outsource all design work. Many large consumer product companies have in-house design teams of several packaging designers yet still outsource design services to fulfill their corporate goals.

The roles and responsibilities of the creative professionals within a design firm or a design group within a consumer product company can vary. Professional experience, expertise, roles, responsibilities and organizational effectiveness all affect the successful outcome of a packaging design. From creative director to production coordinator, every member of the design team must be fully informed of the goals of a specific assignment and the expectations of their role as a team member.

The collaborative role of design is focused not simply on providing outstanding creative services but on meeting clearly defined business objectives, upholding design capabilities, accounting for market-research-based rationales, sourcing appropriate suppliers and vendors, and managing budget and financial requirements.

CHIEF EXECUTIVE OFFICER (CEO)/PRINCIPAL/PARTNER
- Leads the organization
- Develops organizational goals, operating plans, and policies
- Defines short- and long-range business objectives
- Directs and coordinates all managerial activities
- Accounts for budget, finance, and profit and return on capital
- Delegates responsibility and authority

CHIEF CREATIVE OFFICER (CCO)/CREATIVE DIRECTOR/ART DIRECTOR
- Manages client design expectations
- Works actively with the marketing team
- Coordinates the creative team
- Generates and presents strategic concepts
- Maintains accountability of quality, deadlines, and budget parameters
- Accounts for all creative deliverables

This position usually requires a minimum of at least eight years of comprehensive experience, including at least four years in a managerial role, with hands-on design experience, and proven ability to oversee a creative team. A mid- to large-size firm may have more than one creative director. In these organizations the design directors have the same responsibilities within their own team of designers.

DIRECTOR OF CLIENT SERVICES/ACCOUNT EXECUTIVE
- Represents the firm to the client
- Serves as a liaison between the client and the designers
- Communicates with both the design team and the client regarding objectives, strategy, budget, and service-related matters
- Writes marketing plans, proposals, and case studies
- Presents firm capabilities and projects

- Manages workload
- Prioritizes business and marketing services

PRODUCTION MANAGER/COORDINATOR

- Ensures that the design is produced in a high-quality, efficient, and cost-effective manner
- Determines and manages the production budget and necessary resources
- Maintains production schedules
- Establishes printing procedures and quality standards
- Manages production software and work-flow utilities
- Creates mechanicals in spot-color, four-color process, or multicolor processes
- Troubleshoots electronic issues (file creation and management)
- Proofreads and generates files for routing and approval
- Approves printing

STUDIO MANAGER

- Manages the design studio
- Maintains supplies and materials
- Reviews schedules
- Establishes internal project goals
- Assigns projects
- Ensures smooth work flow
- Determines project schedules
- Oversees the quality of work produced
- Coordinates release of presentation and finished work
- Serves as liaison to outside vendors
- Coordinates project-related services and materials

SENIOR DESIGNER

- Provides overall creative direction aimed at planning, creating, and producing packaging designs
- Interprets the client's needs, vision, and strategy
- Understands all aspects of marketing a consumer product
- Articulates client requests and translates creative briefs
- Creates and presents visual presentations
- Supports the writing of creative briefs
- Accounts for the interpretation of brand strategy and architecture
- Prioritizes and manages multiple deadlines including the entire design and development process
- Researches consumer needs and trends

- Develops concepts and color schemes, and turns design ideas into tangible visual commodities
- Establishes the conceptual and stylistic direction for creative work
- Leads, coordinates, and oversees junior design staff and freelance resources
- Coordinates illustration, photography, pre-press, and production, printers, suppliers, and vendors
- Oversees art direction of photo shoots
- Attends press checks
- Budgets expenses
- Interacts and effectively communicates with all levels of the organization

Requirements include a four-year degree in packaging design or another communication design discipline plus at least four to six years of relevant industry experience.

DESIGNER/JUNIOR DESIGNER

- Supports all aspects of the design teams
- Executes senior designer ideas
- Researches materials, resources, competition, and marketing trends
- Assists in presentation development
- Conceptualizes innovative and creative ideas
- Plans, creates, sketches, and produces innovative design concepts
- Works proficiently on the computer using state-of-the-art graphics software
- Develops typographic solutions
- Produces presentation comps

Requirements include a four-year degree in packaging design or another communication design discipline, an exceptional portfolio, and demonstration of computer proficiency in applying current design software.

INDEPENDENT DESIGN CONSULTANT/FREELANCER

- Services the needs of clients
- Produces conceptual strategic design solutions
- Multitasks and prioritizes work
- Manages tight deadlines
- Writes proposals
- Develops and meets budget goals

MARKETING MANAGER

- Directs and oversees all marketing activities
- Develops marketing strategy
- Evaluates marketing environments and prospects
- Makes recommendations for potential services or products

- Defines project development process
- Conducts research
- Synthesizes consumer data
- Sources consumer insights relating to product and packaging technologies
- Plans and guides the strategic direction of a project
- Motivates the teams

BRAND MANAGER
- Directs all aspects of marketing programs for specified product(s)
- Develops and executes marketing strategies
- Directs advertising, packaging design, and all promotional activities related to the brand
- Responsible for hiring and conducting research
- Sources, organizes, and manages design objectives
- Evaluates new products
- Ensures the success of the brand

CONSUMER PSYCHOLOGIST
- Applies the science of psychology to the consumer products arena
- Researches, examines, and explores issues affecting consumer opinions and reactions, from purchasing decisions to shopping patterns
- Provides services to support both the design and the business aspects of understanding marketing strategies

MARKET RESEARCH PROFESSIONAL
- Manages the activities that provide information relating to sales potential and market conditions for a company's products or services
- Directs the investigation of trends
- Explores market developments
- Analyzes sales data
- Provides market recommendations

RESEARCH AND DEVELOPMENT PROFESSIONAL
- Manages research programs and activities to facilitate introduction of new products or processes
- Recommends improvements to existing products or processes
- Gains insights into product improvement and marketing and development opportunities
- Translates research into the development of products for expanding product categories, diversifying product offerings, and for new product openings

INDUSTRIAL DESIGNER/PRODUCT DESIGNER/PACKAGING ENGINEER

- Employs a range of expertise, from creative to engineering skills to design and product shapes and packaging structures
- Solves problems, innovates, and understands how to combine human factors, structural design, materials, and aesthetic appeal
- Works with multidisciplinary and multifunctional teams
- Designs using computer-aided design expertise
- Identifies suitable and available materials
- Assesses manufacturing and production capabilities

SUPPLIER/VENDOR

- Develops technology
- Manufactures packaging structures and closures
- Manufactures packaging and printing materials
- Represents the companies that supply packaging services and materials, including paper, plastics, glass, films, and metals
- Provides services ranging from embossing, die-cutting, prototyping, tooling, converting, and printing
- Works with both clients and designers on packaging technology, machinery, and manufacturing
- Determines and communicates production costs and cycles

Challenges in the Competitive Arena

- Firms or other design teams competing for the same business
- Time management (for example, 10–15 percent is spent on proposal writing and pitching new business)
- Defining the firm's competitive difference/advantage
- Keeping qualified staff
- Maintaining client relationships
- Defining and maintaining standards both within the design team and for the client
- Selling the value of packaging design to clients
- Educating the client on the value of good design
- Operating with a limited budget
- Maintaining sharp communication and presentation skills
- Managing client expectations
- Cultivating the philosophy that packaging design is an investment, not an expense

Communication with the client is among the most critical elements of the process. The design team must always have equanimity with the client. Since many clients do not have a full understanding of the creative process the design team is responsible for keeping the client informed throughout. A successful final outcome and a long-term working relationship can be accomplished only through open, respectful, and professional communication.

Checklist of What Every Designer Needs to Know

✓ **Design**
- Color
- Typography
- Technology/Computer
- Layout
- Pre-Press
- Production
- Printing
- Structural design

✓ **Marketing**
- Demographics
- Consumer Psychology
- Cultural Ethnography
- Retail Design
- Visual Merchandising
- Communication
  Interpersonal
  Presentation
  Verbal
  Written
- Business Skills
- Proposal Writing
- Budgeting
- Billing
- Finance
- Taxes

Excellent communication skills, which include speaking, listening, and writing are required at every professional level, from selling an idea to directing the printer. In addition to the above checklist, communicating using the appropriate professional language, conveying information clearly and directly, and being charismatic, honest, imaginative, smart, energetic, collaborative, dedicated, enthusiastic, ambitious, and passionate are required skills for professional advancement.

✓ DESIGNER DO'S	✗ DESIGNER DON'TS
■ Demonstrate a strategic advantage: Walk the walk and talk the talk	■ Break a deadline
■ Be objective	■ Create obstacles
■ Be a visionary	■ Plagiarize
■ Be a problem solver	
■ Be accurate	
■ Provide options	
■ Make it producible	
■ Add value	
■ Deliver on time	

Strategic Services

Many design firms provide ancillary strategic services that go beyond the design of the consumer product, including brand strategy, consumer research, name generation, point-of-purchase design, structural design and retail design, and global strategic positioning. Since many firms have similar organizational structures, provide similar services, and follow comparable processes, additional services enable them to demonstrate their marketable differences to clients, diversify their client offerings, demonstrate their role as strategic advisor to clients, and present a competitive advantage. Packaging design firms must have professionals that represent a diverse range of expertise to fully support these capabilities.

Design firms or consultancies that have developed ancillary client services generally sell them as "proprietary strategic services." This defines the service as their unique and ownable offering. These services can serve to define a process of design, research, name, symbol, or nomenclature generation, or design analysis.

PRECISE STRATEGIC SERVICE

The following example communicates the language that a design firm would use to sell this type of service to a client.

Precise (usually the design firm gives the service a catchy name) is a comprehensive predesign analysis system. Precise is one of the most vital tools marketers can employ to achieve their brand identity goals. The design firm conducts this extremely thorough analysis before designs are created. With Precise, key marketing information is translated into the design objectives that will maximize every opportunity for success.

The Precise process includes:

Collecting and interpreting pertinent background information such as existing research, positioning strategy, sales data, market trends, advertising, promotion, and merchandising. Data is translated into a meaningful framework for the design process.

A broad visual assessment of the current market environment by the project team to uncover strengths, weaknesses, and opportunities.

An individualized visual assessment of the client's image and communication as well as that of major competitors. If the project involves redesign, this also includes detailed analysis of the current identity with emphasis on existing equities.

Consumer research that utilizes proprietary techniques developed by the firms, which are sensitive to both design and research considerations. The research typically is qualitative in nature and is supervised by the marketing services within the firm. By incorporating the research techniques, the view of the target consumer is an integral part of the process.

The process culminates with a written report and a presentation that details the analysis, providing the critical information for a successful design program.

Strategic services quantify the process for the client into marketable, comprehensible objectives. Although the phraseology and marketing of these services may make them appear vacuous, they provide a framework around what can be an intangible design process.

ANCILLARY STRATEGIC SERVICES CAN INCLUDE:

- Name Generation
- Ideation
- Comprehensive Pre-Design Analysis
- Quantitative Packaging Design Research
- Strategic Marketing Orientation
- Graphic Design Capabilities
- Corporate Identity Capabilities
- Structural Design Services

Categories of Consumer Product Goods

Food and Beverage

Food

Fresh

Prepared

Refrigerated

Frozen

International

Beverage

Soft Drinks

Carbonated

Noncarbonated (flat)

Dairy

Bottled Water

Fruit Juices/Beverages

Wines/Spirits/Beer

Imported

Sports/Energy

Wellness/Nutriceutical

Private Label

Vending

Health and Beauty/Personal Care

Skin Care

Face

Hand/Body

Hair Care

Soaps

Deodorant

Bath

Sun Care

Spa Treatments

Cosmetics

Fragrance

Specialty Items

Pharmaceutical/Medicinal

Vitamins/Diet/Supplements

Herbal

OTC (Over the Counter)

FDA/Prescriptive

Electronics/Technology

Industrial/Automotive

Hardware

Pet Care

Toys/Games/Educational

Entertainment

Luxury Goods

Household Products

Detergents

Paper Goods

Housewares/Home Products

Kitchen

Bath

Bedding

Home Office

Accessories

Lawn/Garden

Sporting Goods

Novelty

Private Label

Non-Retail/Institutional

Professional Profiles

Professional careers vary throughout the business of packaging design. The commonality is the fact that vast challenges are faced daily. From time, personnel, team, and project management to conceptualizing, designing, implementing, producing, and presenting, the day-to-day hurdles and triumphs make for both rewarding and frustrating days. The consummate professional is passionate about his or her work and instills a sense of pride, commitment, and dedication in every undertaking.

The following pages highlight six outstanding design professionals. Their calendars provide a sense of their roles and responsibilities as well as a snapshot of a week in their working lives.

Lisa Francella

Title:	Director
Company:	Pepsi-Cola Design Group
Time in current position:	8 years
Time in profession:	17 years
Education:	BFA School of Visual Arts, New York, NY

SUMMARY OF JOB DESCRIPTION

Manage the Pepsi-Cola Design Group by maximizing creative talent in support of the marketing organization and its various packaging and design initiatives; provide creative design leadership globally; manage trademark equities to ensure global consistency with the marketplace; leverage expertise beyond cross-functional teams within the organization, such as SoBe, Gatorade, Tropicana, et cetera.

SOME OF THE MOST IMPORTANT ASPECTS OF YOUR JOB

Making design recommendations and decisions that ultimately impact consumers in a positive and memorable way; ensuring that design solutions consistently address our marketing objectives and strategic vision; staying ahead of design trends.

TIME FRAME OF A "TYPICAL" PROJECT

2–3 months

Weekly Calendar

Monday

10-11:00 AM : I&U w/ VP PROMOTIONS
11-12:00 PM : WEBSITE PRESENTATION - 5/1 π
2-3:00 PM : WEBSITE RE-WORK SESSION - 5/1 π
3:30-4:00 PM : UPDATE - 2L DESIGN TEST (MY OFFICE)
4:30- 6:00 PM : DISCUSS T1 2006 s/s PROMO/PACKAGING DUPLICATIONS

Tuesday

9-10:00 AM : PROJECT RESTYLE TEAM UPDATE - 5/2 A
11-12:00 PM : STAFF MTG - 5/1 π
3-4:00 PM : RESEARCH MTG.
4:30-5:30 PM : PACKAGING ENHANCEMENT MEETING W/ INNOVATION TEAM - 5/3 A

Wednesday

10-10:30 AM : MEET BEAUTY PACKAGING SUPPLIER
11-12:00 PM : RECAP OF PACKAGING OPPTS. FOR '06
1-2:00 PM : BRAND GRAPHICS REVIEW - 5/1 π
4-5:00 PM : OUTSIDE DESIGN FIRM PRESENTATION - 5/1 π

Thursday

9:30-11:00 AM : DESIGN PRESENTATION TO BRAND GROUP - 5/2 A
11:30-12:00 PM : REVIEW DESIGN CONCEPTS FOR UPCOMING PROMO.
12:00-12:30 PM : DESIGN REVIEW W/ADVERTISING AGENCY - 6/3 BOARDRM.
1-2:30 PM : LUNCH W/ TL @ CENTRO DESIGN
6-7:00 PM : PRESENT CONCEPTS TO CMO & VP COLAS

Friday

8:00-9:00 AM : PREPARE PACKAGING CONCEPTS FOR FINAL PRESENTATION
10-11:00 AM : BOTTLER MTG - 5/1 A
12-12:30 PM : G&A REVIEW
2:30-3:30 PM : GIVE DESIGN FEEDBACK TO MICHELE - ALSO REVIEW REVISED TIMING!
5:30-6:00 PM : DESIGN REVIEW W/ VP COLAS

Notes

- ☑ REMEMBER TO GIVE MARIA FEEDBACK ON HER REVISED DESIGN CONCEPTS
- ☑ SIGN UP FOR DESIGN CONF. IN CHICAGO
- ☑ SET UP MTG. W/ NEW HIRE FROM GC GROUP RE: (MEET N GREET)

Debbie Millman

Title:	President, Design Group
Company:	Sterling Brands Inc.
Time in current position:	2 years; 10 years at Sterling Brands
Time in profession:	12 years in packaging design; 22 years in design
Education:	BA, SUNY Albany; Certificate, Harvard Business School, Business Perspectives for Design Leaders; Milton Glaser Summer Intensive at School of Visual Arts, New York, NY

PERSONAL NOTES

I have had the extreme good fortune of working with amazing clients such as Gillette, Unilever, Kraft, Pfizer, *Star Wars*, the NBA, Nestle, Pepsi, and Campbell's. I am the primary 'rainmaker' for the organization, as well as strategically managing the overall design business and all of our clients.

I also do quite a lot of things "outside" of the office. I am a board member of the New York Chapter of the AIGA and a mentor at the High School of Art and Design. I am also an author on the design blog Speak Up and write for *Print* magazine. This year I began hosting the first weekly radio talk show about design on the Internet. Entitled 'Design Matters with Debbie Millman,' it is featured on the Voice of America Business Network. I also frequently lecture and teach.

TIME FRAME OF TYPICAL PROJECT

From 4 months to 3 years

Weekly Calendar

Monday

- get photos for Met Home deadline

9-10 meeting w/ Simon Williams + Elliott Cato- Growth plan

1:00 meeting w/ Sr. Management team- here at Sterling

2:00-3:00 work on Speak Up article

3:00-4:00 work on Print article for Shelf Life

Tuesday

call Chuck Hardinger

1-2 Dannon Pitch in White Plains case studies, innovation, differentiation

5:00 AIGA Sponsorship Conference Call

7:00 Dinner w/ Pepsi Clients

Wednesday

9-5 Print Business Graphics Design Competition Judging meet Akiko Busch at Print's offices

6- Pamela DeCesare's Birthday (Brand Muse)

Thursday

10-12 meet w/ Stefan Sagmeister (here) - Art project

1:00 Meeting at Adobe
2:30 w/ Ashwini, Alex Isley + Robyn Jordan

3:00 Pepperidge Farm internal meeting
4:00 here

7:00 Dinner w/ Cheryl Swanson / Toniq

Friday

11:00 Conf call w/ SF office re: Pepp farm

12:00 AIGA NY Sponsorship meeting (here)

3:00 Radio Show Voice America Design Matters with Emily Oberman - Number Seventeen

5:00 Drinks w/ Emily Oberman + John Fulbrook from Simon + Schuster

Notes

call Robsham at KC
Darralyn Rieth at CSC
Jan 2099
Bill Cunderman
Amy Bresner
Lisa Francella
Laurence Berger's office

- work on speech for Pamela Paris's intro for AIGA Design Legends Gala

week of August 29

Dean Lindsay

Title: Founder/President

Company: Dean Lindsay Design Inc.

Time in current position: 25 years

Time in profession: 30 years

Education: BS, Medical Illustration;
                               MA, Industrial Design,
                               Ohio State University

PERSONAL NOTES

Founder of a Chicago packaging innovation consultancy providing design leadership for clients in brand development for Fortune 100 companies that includes new business development and strategic design planning for packaging innovation. Responsibilities include staying on top of technological changes in both packaging and design tools, particularly digital applications in design, production, engineering, and prototyping; accountability for each client's business approach; and deliverables for all projects.

TIME FRAME OF TYPICAL PROJECT
4–6 months

Weekly Calendar

Monday

- MEET W/ STAFF - REVIEW PROJECTS (1.5H)
- CONF CALL W/ CLIENT - REVISIONS (1 HR)
- CONF CALL W/ PKG. VENDOR - DISCUSS VOLUMETRIC CALC. FOR BOTTLE DESIGN
- CONF CALL W/ MODEL MAKER - DISCUSS PROTOTYPES FOR CONSUMER RESEARCH
- INTERVIEW IND. DESIGNER FOR JOB (PRODUCTION DESIGNER)
- MEET W/ ADMIN ASST TO REVIEW PROJECT BILLING
- NEW BIZ EMAILS

Tuesday

- POWERPOINT DRAFT FOR THURS. CLIENT MEETING (INCLUDE STRATEGY, RATIONALE)
- CALL CLIENT - CONFIRM MEETING
- CALL FORMER CLIENT (SAME CO.) - REQUEST 30 MIN. 'UPDATE'
- STAFF REVIEW OF DESIGNS FOR THURS. PRESENTATION. FINAL REVISION.
- MEET DESIGN DIRECTOR - DISCUSS NEW PROJECT STRATEGY-TIMING
- NEW BIZ EMAILS
- DINNER W/ PROSPECTIVE CLIENT TO DISUSS NEW BIZ OPPORTUNITY

Wednesday

- FOLLOW UP CALL W/ TUES. DINNER PROSPECT TO DISUSS VIBE
- VISIT LOCAL GROCERY TO REVIEW COMPETITIVE PRODUCTS ON SHELF
- VISIT ART GALLERY (MENTAL FLOSS)
- WORK ON PACK EXPO SPEECH (WHAT DO THEY WANT TO HEAR?)
- TRAVEL FOR CLIENT PRESENTATION - CATCH 5.40 PM FLIGHT (DON'T FORGET LAPTOP & DIGITAL PROJECTOR!)

Thursday

- UP BY 5AM! RENTAL CAR TO CLIENT OFFICE (DON'T FORGET DIRECTIONS)
- ARRIVE CLIENT'S OFFICE - SET UP LAPTOP; WAIT 30 MIN. (REMAIN CALM!)
- MEET CLIENT TEAM. PRESENT DESIGNS. (LISTEN TO RESPONSES; TAKE NOTES)
- MEET FORMER CLIENT - DISUSS FUTURE BIZ OPPORTUNITIES (FACE TIME IS IMPORTANT!)
- REVIEW NOTES ON PLANE; FOLLOW UP EMAILS FOR PRESENTATION & CLIENT CHAT. - ZONK OUT!

Friday

- MORNING CALL (8 AM) TO CLIENT TO REVIEW VIBE FROM THURS. MEETING
- STAFF MEETING TO DEBRIEF ON CLIENT PRESENTATION
- MORNING CALLS TO PROSPECTIVE CLIENTS (FROM 'HIT LIST')
- EMERGENCY CALL FROM MODEL MAKER - FILE CORRUPTED (PASS OFF TO DESIGN DIRECTOR - CROSS FINGERS!)
- CALL INDUSTRIAL DESIGNER FROM MON. INTERVIEW - MAKE OFFER (DECISION BY MON.)

Notes — EVERY DAY:

- BE FLEXIBLE - THINGS CHANGE
- SAVE FRI. FOR SALES TEL. CALLS - PEOPLE USE FRI TO CATCH-UP
- SET EXAMPLE FOR GOOD WORK ETHIC: - IN EARLY, STAY 'TIL 5
- FOSTER CREATIVE / SELF-ACTUALIZING OFFICE ENVIRONMENT
- BE AVAILABLE - NO SHUT DOORS
- EMAILS ARE OK. FACE TIME BETTER
- HAVE FUN - DESIGN IS A CREATIVE LIFE!!

Adrienne Muken

Title:	Designer
Company:	IQ Design Group
Time in current position:	3½ years
Time in profession:	3½ years
Education:	ASS Display and Exhibit Design, BFA Packaging Design, FIT (Fashion Institute of Technology), New York, NY

PERSONAL NOTES

Since I don't work at a huge firm, designers have more responsibilities than most. Besides working on phase one, I'm responsible for all subsequent phases, art directing illustrators, and seeing a project through to production with client interaction and feedback along the way. Ideally a project could enter and leave the studio in three to four weeks. Normally a creative phase one is in the art department for approximately five to seven days. Refinements are usually scheduled for no more than three to four days, with extra time allotted for photo shoots or final illustration as needed. In the midst of this could be focus groups, brainstorming sessions, and meetings with illustrators.

TIME FRAME OF TYPICAL PROJECT

3–4 weeks

Weekly Calendar

Monday

START PHASE 1 DESIGN EXPLOR.
- 'SPEC' TYPE FOR LOGO
- IMAGE SOURCING

CHOOSE SUBSTRATE & SPEC COLORS FOR NEW CANDY DESIGN IN FINAL STAGES OF PRODUCTION

PROVIDE LAYOUTS FOR UPCOMING PHOTOSHOOT

Tuesday

STAFF MEETING TO DISCUSS CURRENT PROJECTS & OFFICE ISSUES

ART DIRECT ILLUSTRATOR FOR FINAL ART TO BE USED IN NUTRITIONAL BAR LAYOUTS

ATTEND FOCUS GROUP FOR OBSERVATION PURPOSES

Wednesday

BRAINSTORMING MEETING FOR NEW "SNACK PACK" PROJECT & IN-HOUSE PROMOTIONAL MAILER

CONFERENCE CALL W/ CLIENT TO DISCUSS PHASE 2 REVISIONS

WITH PRODUCTION TEAM, APPROVE COLOR PROOF FROM PRINTER

Thursday

COORDINATE W/ ACCOUNT MGR. TO DETERMINE HOURS & DELIVERABLE FOR UPCOMING PROJECT

WORK W/ PRODUCTION DEPARTMENT TO HAND OFF FINAL ARTWORK

BRIEF OTHER DESIGNERS ON KNOWLEDGE GAINED FROM CONFERENCE CALL

Friday

ATTEND CLIENT MEETING TO PRESENT PHASE 1 OF NEW CANDY PROJECT

SEND OUT, VIA EMAIL, PHASE 2 REVISIONS WITH A WRITTEN SUMMARY OF CHANGES & STRATEGY

Notes

TO DO:
- ORGANIZE & FILE ALL MY CLIENT EMAILS FROM THIS WEEK
- TAKE CARE OF ADMIN DUTIES (TIME SHEETS!)
- MESSENGER COLOR SWATCHES TO CLIENT

Jason Lombardo

Title: Designer

Company: Spring Design Partners

Time in current position: 1½ years

Time in profession: 1½ years

Education: AAS Communication Design;
                                    BFA, Packaging Design, FIT
                                    (Fashion Institute of Technology),
                                    New York, NY

PERSONAL NOTES

Summary of job description in designing consumer brands includes creative ideation and sketching, structural exploration, custom typography, illustration, building preproduction files, comping, client presentations, photography direction, executing layouts/design sketches, research, retouching, and developing visual language and style guides. The most important part of the job is client interaction, ideation, and executing creative concepts in a timely manner.

TIME FRAME OF TYPICAL PROJECT

For phase one: 1–2 weeks;
From client brief to postproduction: 3–6 months

Weekly Calendar

Monday

1 hour Work-in-Progress meeting
2 ½ hours Retouching Food Photography
1 ½ hours sketching for
  layouts of new snack food.
2 hours creating illustration for
  microwave instructions for frozen
  meal product
1.5 hours executing design layouts
½ hour researching upcoming
  project

Tuesday

1 ½ hours of research (internet based)
4 hours of concept development,
  sketches, preliminary designs
  for a health/nutrition line of
  products, redesign
1 hour revisions to layout of a
  health snack food product.
1 ½ hours executing selected design
  concepts.
1 ½ hours developing typography for
  product names in a snack line

Wednesday

2 hours developing promotional
  packaging for a beverage line.
2 hours creating a digital illustration
  of what a clubstore palette
  would look like with our new designs,
  for a snack food line.
1 hour creating web homepages and
  landing pages for promotional purposes
  for beverage line.
1 ½ hours preparing for presentation
  (boards, review, shelf sets, etc.)
2 hours Revisions of new designs for snack
  line.
1 hour developing visual for cracker product

Thursday

3 hours developing concepts, sketches
  and layouts for a tobacco product, redesign.
1 ½ hours executing from sketches
  to layout for a wood-care product, new line.
½ hour meeting, new project brief
1 ½ hour brainstorming session for
  originals structures for a new product.
1 hour design meeting - critique for
  tobacco product redesign.
1 hour working on revisions/direction
  from critique.

Friday

1 hour re-working layout/design for
  'pet food' product
1 ½ hour design critique for wood-care
  product.
3 ½ hours developing visual language
  ideas/concepts for a new beverage
  product launch.
1 hour designing icons for a liquor
  product
1 hour reviewing and revising visual
  language concepts.

Notes

Out of office days include
client presentations and
art-directing photo shoots
for food photography & product
or prop photography. As well
as researching in retail environments and shops.

75

Carson Ahlman

Title:	Industrial Design Consultant
Company:	Carson Ahlman Design
Time in current position:	17 years
Time in profession:	22 years
Education:	BS, Industrial Design,
	University of the Arts, Philadelphia, PA

PERSONAL NOTES

I am a creative industrial design resource for agencies, manufacturers, and marketers of a wide variety of consumer brands. I specialize in concept, creation, and development of POP (point of purchase) displays, structural packaging, and product design. My interpretations of brand equities are incorporated into the dimensional components of a structure and help to bring a holistic and memorable presentation to the consumer.

Responsibilities include creatively uniting marketing objectives with problem solving solutions that incorporate manufacturing situations with the latest materials and processes. My development process, which begins with visualization skills, is refined by utilizing various digital/engineering applications and prototypes that culminates in a unified, brand presentation.

TIME FRAME OF TYPICAL PROJECT
1–2 weeks

Weekly Calendar

Monday

MEET W/ BRAND CONSULTANTS ABOUT VAC-FORMS FOR CELL PHONES 9:30

FINISH SKETCHES FOR FLOOR DISPLAY FOR NEW NOIR PRODUCT

CONDUCT RETAIL AUDIT FOR LIQUOR BOTTLES

FINISH FOAM CORE OF INTERACTIVE KIOSK AND DEL. 4:30

Tuesday

DEVELOP CONCEPTS FOR CELL PHONE VAC-FORM.

DEL. FLOOR DISPLAY SKETCHES TO DISPLAY MANUFACTURER. 2:30

CREATE BOTTLE DESIGNS FOR TEQUILA PRODUCT B/W SKETCHES

DEVELOP CONTROL DRAWING FOR KIOSK UNIT E-MAIL TO JIM

Wednesday

DEVELOP 3D IMAGES OF SELECTED FLOOR DISPLAYS DEL. FRI. 11:00

DEL. CELL PHONE VAC-FORM CONCEPTS START 3D DATA FILES FOR MODELS

FINISH TEQUILA BOTTLE DESIGNS

CREATE DIE LINES OF PAPER BOARD INSERTS FOR VAC-FORMS

Thursday

E-MAIL 3D DATA FILES TO MODEL MAKER + REVIEW

FINISH TEQUILA BOTTLE DESIGNS AND DEL. 2:00

MEET W/ DISPLAY CO. ABOUT END CAP DISPLAY FOR OFFICE PRODUCTS 4:30

TYPE + E-MAIL INVOICES

Friday

DEL. 3D IMAGES OF FLOOR DISPLAY E-MAIL TO SUSAN

TAKE MEASUREMENTS AT STAPLES OF END CAP

PRESENT PORTFOLIO TO NEW BRANDING FIRM 2:30

Notes

4 DESIGN FUNDAMENTALS

Basic Design Principles

Knowledge of the fundamental principles of two-dimensional design is an essential component to any visual problem-solving assignment. Basic design principles, as they relate to the use of design elements such as line, shape, color, and texture, provide guidelines that shape visual communication and the ability to maneuver through the packaging design process.

Two-dimensional design begins with an understanding of a layout, which is the purposeful arrangement of design elements to form the visual communication. The key objective of a layout is to create a visual organization that is satisfying, stimulating, thought-provoking, and pleasing to the eye. Some layouts follow a grid (a framework that provides a fixed system for the layout), while others are guided by analyzing the design elements and how they function in their respective positions. The first step toward this goal is to understand design principles, how design elements are affected by their relationship to one another, and how this impacts the overall visual communication.

There are varying concepts relating to the basic principles of design. They can be specific as they relate to a distinct discipline or can be general as they refer to compositional guidelines. The principles defined here can significantly enhance the understanding of what makes one packaging design layout work while another seems unresolved.

■ **Balance**
Balance is the convergence of elements or parts to create a design that makes the appearance of a "whole." Visual balance can be created by symmetry or asymmetry.

■ **Contrast**
Contrast is created when elements are placed in a way that emphasizes their differences. Contrast can be in the form of weight, size, scale, color, value, or the positive and negative dynamics of space.

■ **Tension**
Tension is the balance of opposing elements. A layout that utilizes the principle of tension can stimulate visual interest by giving one element greater stress or emphasis.

■ **Positive and Negative**
Positive and negative refers to the opposing relationship of design elements in a composition. The object or element constitutes the positive, and the space or environment in which the element exists is the negative.

■ **Value**
Value is created by lightness or darkness of color. Applying the principle of value is a useful way to control the viewer's attention through contrasts of light and dark.

■ **Weight**
Weight refers to the size, shape, and color of a visual in relation to other elements.

■ **Position**
Position is the placement of elements in relation to one another within the visual format. Position creates a focal point that in turn guides the viewer's eye.

■ **Alignment**
Alignment is the arrangement of visual elements in logical groupings that are comfortable to human perception and visually support the flow of information.

■ **Hierarchy**
Hierarchy is created by the organization of visual elements in steps or ranks by their order of importance. The level of dominance given to elements can be visually communicated by size, weight, value, position, alignment, and scale.

■ **Texture**
A two-dimensional composition can communicate texture through the use of design styles. Texture can give a composition depth or can simulate physical qualities such as smooth, coarse, or grainy.

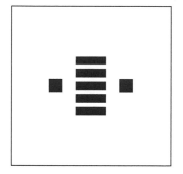

small

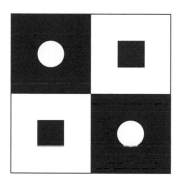

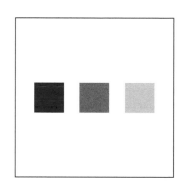

heavy **WEIGHT**

LIGHT WEIGHT

The focal point could be positioned anywhere within the format depending on the communication

your eye starts/stops here

dominant communication point ▬▬▬

secondary communication aligns flush left with dominant communication point

tertiary communication aligns flush left with graphic element

Illustrations of basic design principles

Packaging Design Principles

In packaging design the basic design principles are customized to meet the objectives of each design assignment. These guidelines help to define how color, typography, structure, and imagery are applied within a design layout to create the right sense of balance, tension, proportion, and appeal. This is what makes the design elements form the communicative attributes of the packaging design.

There are numerous variables that affect how and why packaging design attracts consumers. Consumer researchers spend countless hours analyzing these variables. From a purely design perspective (removing other marketing variables such as price, location, and brand loyalty) there are significant elements that best capture consumer attention and break through the visual clutter of the retail environment.

Top Four Attention Grabbers:

- Color
- Physical Structure or Shape
- Symbols and Numbers
- Typography

The attraction of design elements is based on:

Basic principles of design + clear marketing objectives + effective use of top four attention grabbers = well-designed consumer packaging design

Packaging design that serves the intended target market should be:

- Culturally appropriate
- Linguistically accurate
- Visually logical
- Competitively designed

The Primary Display Panel

No matter what the structure of the packaging design is or what material it is made from (a bottle, jar, cylinder, tube, bag, pouch, or box), there is an area reserved for the brand identity and the primary communication elements. This area, called the principle or Primary Display Panel (PDP), is considered the front of the packaging design. The size and shape of the PDP constitutes the display area for the most important visual aspect of the packaging design: the visual communication of the marketing and brand strategy. The PDP holds a significant share of the responsibility in selling the packaging design in the crowded retail environment.

Tahitian Noni TePoema

Client: Tahitian Noni
Design Firm:
Hornall Anderson
Design Works
Designers:
Jack Anderson,
Lisa Cerveny,
James Tee,
Tiffany Place,
Leo Raymundo,
Jana Nishi,
Elmer dela Cruz,
Bruce Branson-
Meyer

Hierarchy is the emphasis or dominance of elements or typography to show order of communication. When hierarchy is correct, the eye follows the design through a comfortable logical sequence.

Kashi TLC Crackers

Client:
Kashi Company
Design Firm:
Addis Design
Creative Director/
Designer:
Joanne Hom

The personality of this well-designed, playful PDP effectively captures attention and communicates the product's benefits.

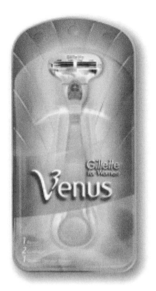
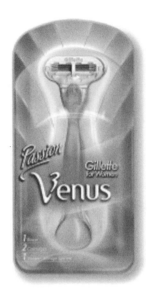
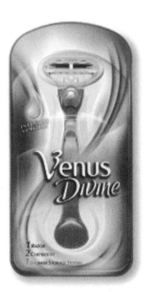

Venus
Client:
The Gillette
Company
Design Firm:
Wallace Church
Creative Director:
Stan Church
Designers:
John Bruno,
Lawrence Haggerty
(logo), Paula Bunny

A well-designed
PDP may be a
simple, clean
design that clearly
communicates
the product's
personality.

Required elements generally include:

- Brand Mark
- Brand Name
- Product Name
- Ingredient Copy
- Net Weight
- Nutritional Information
- Expirations, Hazards, Directions, Dosage, Instructions
- Variety
- Bar Code

Elements dictated by design include:

- Colors
- Imagery
- Characters
- Illustrations
- Graphic Devices
- Photographs (noninformational)
- Symbols (noninformational)
- Icons
- Visual Hierarchy

Understanding the order of importance of primary and secondary design elements helps to determine their distribution on the packaging design. Generally speaking, the primary elements can consist of the ones that are required by the marketer, by a regulatory authority, or by an assessment of the most important communication elements. Secondary elements comprise all supplementary design elements, such as product descriptors or romance copy. The size, position, and relationship of the elements are determined by basic layout and design principles, and a hierarchical system is used in overall strategy of the packaging design. The hierarchy of information is successful when the design is easy to read, meaning the eyes move around the design reading what is most important first and following around in a logical sequence.

Hierarchy and clear communication:

- Elements are organized by importance.
- Information can be clearly understood.
- Variety, assortment, and product differences are easy to distinguish.

The Well-Designed PDP

- Communicates the marketing/brand strategy effectively
- Illustrates product information clearly
- Emphasizes information by hierarchy and is uncluttered and easy to read
- Suggests the function, usage, and purpose visually
- Describes the usage and directions effectively
- Differentiates the product from the competition
- Distinguishes the product on the shelf and in relation to other varieties

5 TYPOGRAPHY

Typography and Packaging Design

In packaging design, typography is the primary medium for the communication of the product's name, function, and facts to a broad consumer audience. The typographic selection, layout, and treatment of the words and letterforms effect how the type is read. Ultimately the typography on a packaging design becomes one of the most significant elements of the visual expression of the product.

Typography derives from the Greek roots of *typos* ("impression") and *graphein* ("to write"). Typography is the use of letterforms to visually communicate a verbal language. Since letterforms are shaped by the culture in which they exist, their use for typographic means is part of a culture's visual language. As type designer Eric Gill, in his book *An Essay on Typography*, stated, "Letters are things, not pictures of things."

Typographic forms can be letterforms or individual characters, words, shapes, or symbols. Readability, legibility, reading time (how long it takes someone to read), size, shape, and style are all characteristics of typography that affect communication. In particular, both the mechanics of reading (for example, from left to right and visa versa) and individual perception have a significant effect on the communication of typography.

Categories of Type

Traditionally an understanding of type categories helped designers recognize similarities and distinguishable characteristics between groups of typestyles. These categories enabled designers to make selections appropriately for text, headings, and other copy. With the thousands of digital typefaces available today and the extensive use of typography as a means of expression, designers no longer need to search for typestyles based on traditional categorization. New technology-based font management and organization software as well as search engines that allow for the input of descriptions such as "warm," "cold," "feminine," "bold," and "light" to generate an extensive list of fonts that match the style, enable the designer to maneuver through the thousands of available typestyles. Although these software tools make sorting typography by style easier, designers must be careful not to devalue their design expertise and allow technology to make their design decisions.

A basic understanding of typestyle categories and their design attributes can facilitate the selection process.

Old Style fonts include Times New Roman, Bembo, Palatino, Goudy, New Baskerville, Garamond, and Janson. They:

- resemble the hand lettering of scribes;
- are graceful in appearance;
- have a low contrast (the thick and thin strokes are not very different from each other);
- have serifs on lowercase letters that are slanted;
- have serifs that are bracketed;
- have a main stroke that is curved, not sharp;
- are a good choice for a lengthy body of text.

Modern/Serif fonts include Bodoni, Times, Fenice, and Madrone. They have:

- high-contrasting thicks and thins that are radically different;
- thin parts of the letters as the vertical stresses;
- serifs that are horizontal, unbracketed, and meet the stroke with a sharp angle.

Slab Serif/Egyptian/Square Serif fonts include Clarendon, New Century Schoolbook, Memphis, Rockwell, and Aachen. They have:

- little or no contrast between the thick and thin strokes;
- vertical lines that are stressed;
- serifs that consist of thick horizontal slabs.

Sans Serif fonts include Avant Garde, Gill Sans, Franklin Gothic, Frutiger, Helvetica, and Futura. They have:

- no serifs;
- tall X-heights (lowercase letter heights);
- no contrast or vertical stresses;
- no difference in stroke weight either vertical or horizontal.

Script fonts include Zapf Chancery and Edwardian Decorative. They:

- resemble handwriting or calligraphy;
- have large initial caps.

Decorative fonts:

- have an aesthetic decorative style;
- are not necessarily designed for readability.

Although decorative fonts have expressive styles, they should be used with caution in packaging design since they can appear trendy, ornamental, or overly stylized. The designer must be discriminating with typographic choices and discern the broad visual communication purpose of a font before using it.

UPPER AND LOWERCASE

In the days of early typesetters, characters were printed from metal molds; and when not in use, the molds were stored in wooden trays. The uppercase tray contained capital letters that were not used as frequently; the lowercase one contained small letters. Hence the origin of the terms *uppercase* and *lowercase*.

Typography and Technology

Technology has greatly reshaped every aspect of packaging design including the use of typography. Since the professional typesetter no longer exists, the role of the designer has expanded to include typographic mastery. With global access to computers, designers have access to thousands of digital fonts. However, the art of typography can be easily lost with the use of technology and type hacked out without artful care. The designer should focus on typography as a means of communication that is affected by the visual arrangement of words, letters, and styles.

In packaging design, the need for consistent high-quality reproduction is critical; therefore, only high-quality fonts should be used. High-quality typefaces provide complete families and character sets that include different weights—light, regular, bold, heavy—and different styles—roman, italic, condensed. Fonts must have superior digitization, optimal on-screen depiction, meticulous laser-printing quality, and exceptional reproduction quality. The details of letters, including shapes and outlines, must not be broken or disturbed, and the screen legibility of the font must always match print legibility. Be warned that although a typeface may seem to be the original classic font (Bodoni, Garamond, and Caslon), many of these have been copied, altered, and then redesigned. Although these fonts may be more affordable, they can be of inferior quality and may not be best for client use.

Keeping track of the range of typefaces available for any design problem can be overwhelming. Creating a printed library is a way to catalog fonts for easy access. Using font-management software is essential in creating digital design files. By relying on a core group of favorite classic typefaces and using innovation, creativity, and typographic sensitivity, a designer can turn any classic typeface into an exciting and original logo for a brand or product name.

Typography and Kerning

Kerning is the adjustment of space between letters of a word to make them appear visually unified. Depending on the side-by-side appearance of each letter (the white

Kerning
The space between each letter should be adjusted to make the overall word have a more cohesive and visually appealing appearance.

too tight

too loose

uniform kerning

typography

tracked too tight

space between the edge of one letter and the edge of another), there may be more space on one side of a letter and less on the other. Adjusting these gaps between adjacent letters establishes visual harmony.

Although most computer programs have internal font-kerning systems, the automatic spacing does not always create visually pleasing or perfect kerning. Graphic software and page layout programs allow for manual kerning, giving designers the opportunity to determine proportional spacing between each character. Ultimately it is the designers' responsibility to examine each word and letter, and individually resolve kerning and line-spacing issues. Proper kerning supports the aesthetic success of a packaging design.

To determine where kerning is visually necessary:

- Turn the word upside down. This takes away the subjective appearance of the word since it is difficult to separate how it is read from how it is seen. Once the word is upside down, the positive and negative spaces between the letters are seen more clearly. Each letter can now be examined in relation to adjacent letters rather than as the whole word.

- Put the word up on a wall and stand back from it. Although adjustments may be necessary in smaller font sizes, in packaging design kerning is more critical in larger font sizes, where the audience is viewing the type from a distance. From a distance gaps between letters are more obvious.

- Squint your eyes to see forms rather than letters.

- Zoom in and out on every two letters on the computer screen. This helps to see the visual letter spacing much like standing back from the wall.

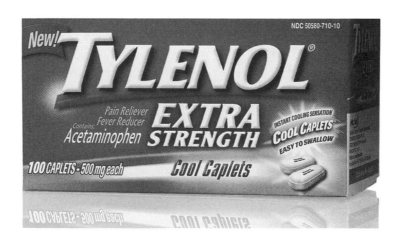

Tylenol
Client:
McNeil Consumer
and Specialty
Pharmaceuticals
Design Firm:
Colemanbrandworx
(CBX)
Designer:
Peter Chieffo

Kerning letters that do not necessarily fit well together can be difficult. The Tylonol logo illustrates effective kerning.

Typographic Principles for Packaging Design

The typographic rules that apply to other printed mediums—such as type size, use of capital letters, use of decorative typefaces, typographic alignment, spacing, kerning, and hyphenation—are not necessarily the same rules that apply in packaging design. Since typography for packaging design serves to communicate the marketing message on a three-dimensional medium and is initially viewed from a distance by people of varying cultural, social, and ethnic backgrounds in a short amount of time, typographic rules are guided by each individual assignment.

Typography for packaging design must be:

- readable and legible from a few feet away;
- designed to the scale and shape of the three-dimensional structure;
- understandable by a diverse audience;
- credible and informative in the communication of product information.

Different than on two-dimensional forms of communication, such as magazines or books, the typographic composition in packaging design is not formulaic in the use of a grid system. The typographic architecture varies for every packaging design and is determined by factors that include the package's shape and size, product description, category competition, retail environment, shelf positioning, and regulatory requirements.

These principles provide a framework for typographic decision making for packaging design.

Principle 1: Define the Typographic Personality

The typography must work to define the packaging design's personality. The visual personality is what communicates how consumers perceive a design. Research, experimentation, proper type selection (font, size, and weight), and a clear visual communication strategy provide the foundation.

Principle 2: Limit Typefaces

Give careful consideration to how many typefaces are needed to communicate a concept. Three typefaces is a general limit for any primary display panel in packaging design. Sometimes it is difficult to limit the number of typefaces because of the quantity of copy required. In this case it is best to employ typefaces that offer a variety of styles within the same family; this provides a clear, consistent appearance and a unified message.

Principle 3: Create Typographic Hierarchy

Typographic hierarchy, the organization of the visual information, provides the framework for how information is "read" from greater to lesser importance—this is

Mrs. Meyer's
A strong brand personality can be achieved with limited typestyles.

how the consumer knows at a quick glance what to "get" from a packaging design. Typographic elements are ranked in their order of importance; and with the use of design principles such as positioning, alignment, relationship, scale, weight, contrast, and color, the typographic hierarchy is developed to meet the visual communication objective.

Hierarchy can be created by grouping related items together and spacing unrelated items farther apart. When clustered, words or groups of words communicate as a unit. All typography on a packaging design must be situated with a purpose, and the type choice and layout should support the design concept. Typographic elements should be positioned in terms of how they relate to one another—directly, indirectly, or not at all.

Principle 4: Define the Typographic Positioning

Typographic positioning is the physical placement of the typography within the primary display area: the individual location of letters, words, and bodies of text in relation to other design elements.

Principle 5: Determine Font Alignment

Alignment defines the overall architecture of the layout. The alignment of each word on a packaging design should be carefully considered since words that are centered, flush left, flush right, or justified communicate differently. The shape of the packaging structure dictates the organization of the layout and the appropriate alignment choices.

Post Cereals
Client:
Post Cereals/
Kraft Foods
Design Firm:
Sterling Brands
Designer:
Sterling Studio

Typographic hierarchy, positioning, and contrast.

Basic typographic alignments can be:

- **centered**—with each word or line of copy centered within the primary display panel or a specific area;
- **flush left**—with each word or line of copy aligned on the left, used most often in Western cultures, where reading is from left to right;
- **flush right**—with each word or line of copy aligned on the right, can be an awkward choice when there is a significant amount of copy for consumers to read;
- **justified**—with words or lines of copy stretched to the same width, but here letter and word spacing can be challenging.

Principle 6: Vary Typographic Scale

In typography, *scale* usually refers to the enlargement or reduction of point size (that of the character). In typography for packaging design, it refers to the size relationships of typographic elements in relation to one another. For example, brand identities (brand names, their logos, etc.) are generally bigger in scale than the product descriptor (or product variety). All copy on the front or primary display panel of a package must be scaled to a size that is legible from a short distance—that between the consumer and the package on the shelf in the retail environment. Typographic scale should always be appropriate to other elements and to the overall size of the package. Scale relates to emphasis; consider positioning and alignment along with scale.

Tecni.art
Client: L'Oréal
Design Firm:
Bergman
Associates NYC
Designer:
Robert Bergman

In this completely typographic packaging design the scale of the brand name creates visual impact.

Principle 7: Choose to Contrast

Contrasting typefaces is one means to communicate words or lines of copy that may be equally important but distinctly different. Typographic contrast—light vs. bold, italic vs. roman, serif vs. san serif—allows the designer to organize information for the consumer and add interest to the layout. For type contrast to be effective, the two words or groups of words must look obviously different and intentional. Creating contrast that is not easily apparent is purposeless.

Principle 8: Experiment with Type

There are no hard and fast rules to guide the designer's typographic exploration process. Experimenting with typestyles, characters, letterforms, ligatures, kerning, and layout is an important part of the design process. This enables the designer to come up with a greater range of distinctive solutions. Experimentation is the part of the creative exercise that allows ideas to be visualized and take shape. The process is a critical evolutionary step toward the success of a final design solution.

Steel Reserve and Steel Six Cans
Client: Steel Brewing Company/McKenzie River
Design Firm: Turner Duckworth
Creative Director: David Turner, Bruce Duckworth
Designer: David Turner
Account Manager: Joanne Chan

Typographic contrast can increase visual impact.

Principle 9: Stack Characters Carefully

The general rule in packaging design is not to stack type. Stacking characters and letters on top of one another in a vertical line does not work well in Western cultures, where letterforms are read horizontally. The ascenders and descenders of

lowercase letters do not sit on top of each other properly, which diminishes readability. Stacked characters on a packaging design can make shelf stocking confusing since the proper vertical or horizontal orientation for the product is unclear. Although there are cases in which this design choice works, stacking type should be considered carefully.

Yamas/Student Project
Designer:
Jennifer Tsavos/FIT (Fashion Institute of Technology)

Stack type carefully.

Principle 10: Remove Your Visual Bias

Since every designer perceives visuals in a different context, it is important that the designer's personal preferences do not interfere with his or her typographic experiments. Although some designers may believe that what makes for creativity in design is intuition, the professional process should not be based on "I knew it would work" or "I like that font" decision making. Designers should be able to explain their design process and their rationale for typographic solutions, and the packaging design must ultimately stand on its own.

LEAVE TYPOGRAPHIC DESIGN TO A PROFESSIONAL

Type design is a specialized field. The development of precisely proportioned letterforms is a time-consuming art. Type designers take great pains to create each individual letter so that all work together to achieve a balanced presentation throughout the entire font. With the millions of typefaces to choose from, packaging designers should avoid creating their own fonts unless the look is intentional. Although certain handwritten styles can be the defining personality of a brand, when using handwritten styles they must be refined and balanced both in character weight and kerning.

Principle 11: Make It Ownable

The brand name and the product name are what the consumer connects to both mentally and emotionally, so the typography used should be unique to the brand as well as *ownable*. This can be achieved without creating a whole new typeface or designing one by hand. Using an existing typeface, characters can be revised, new letterforms can be designed, ligatures can be created, and type can be skewed for an "italic" style. However, caution should be taken to maintain the integrity of the original type design.

Whether a single character is changed or the entire font is modified, the goal is to create a typographic solution that is easily identifiable with the specific product or brand. Marketers recognize that it is often the uniqueness of the type that makes for brand distinction.

Principle 12: Be Consistent

Consistent use of type in personality, style, positioning, and hierarchy creates a unified look across a brand family or line of product, creating a strong shelf presence. In addition, the consistent use of typography can help to build brand equity because the consumer comes to identify the typographic style with the brand.

Principle 13: Refinement for Typographic Excellence

Refinement is the process of examining and modifying the typography with typographic excellence as the goal. The development of a brand logo can take a considerable amount of time to perfect. Attention should be paid to every detail including the shape of the letterforms, kerning, ligatures and the overall typographic personality. Typographic refinement is essential to the quality of the end result. Ultimately typographic excellence is achieved when the type has clear expressive power that impacts the packaging design in a way that makes an immediate impression on the consumer and sparks a transaction.

H2Oh! Sparkling Water
Client: Pepsi-Cola
Design Firm:
Cuticone Design
Art Director(s):
Pepsi-Cola Design
Group:
Adriana Columbo,
Michelle Witenko
Designer:
Joe Cuticone,
Diane Lamendola

Make the brand
identity "ownable."

Designing the Brand Identity

In packaging design it is the brand identity that begins the visual and verbal story, and brings life to the brand and its products. In this regard, typography contributes immensely to the representation of a brand through its logo. The development of a logo is an extensive process that is critical to the packaging design's success. This dynamic process can take a significant length of time. From design strategy, concept development, typographic choice, final design solution, to implementation there is an extensive amount of typographic design and tweaking that takes place.

Typographic considerations for the brand identity are not unlike those for other aspects of the packaging design; however, since significant investment is made in the product's name, it is through the logo that the character of the product makes its first and most lasting impression. Stroke weights, letter heights, kerning, spacing, ligatures, outlines, colors, and symbols should be fine-tuned every step of the way. The process of brand identity design similarly follows the phases outlined in Chapter 10. Additional considerations for the brand identity include future design applications, printing specifications, color combinations, and symbol or icon use with and without type. A design standards manual is a way to provide guidelines for the application of the brand identity and to establish acceptable and unacceptable uses.

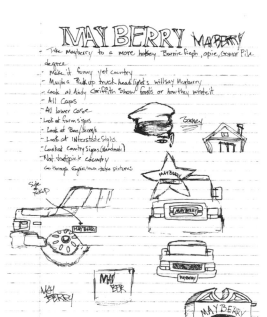

 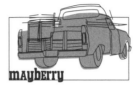

**Mayberry
Brand Identity
Development/
Student Project**
(spread)
Designer:
Jason Offsey/FIT
(Fashion Institute
of Technology)

Initial sketches and
logo development
for a brand identity
immediately suggest
the personality of the
Mayberry market.

Brand/Product Name

There are times when the brand name and the product name are one and the same. Generally speaking, the product name is the most important typography on the packaging design. Not unlike a person's name, this is the visual that the consumer will identify with the product, similar to a person's signature. Type choice, scale, positioning, layout, color, and design should all function to communicate the personality of the product.

Secondary Copy

Positioning and alignment of secondary copy is dependent on the hierarchy of other more predominant elements. Typically it follows the brand name and/or the product name. Secondary copy that reads in text blocks should have line breaks that keep logical words together and be of a width that makes it easy to read. When a line of copy is too long the reader may lose his or her place and have to reread; any excessively long copy line should be shortened appropriately. The type choice for secondary copy should complement or contrast the product name.

Product Descriptor

Descriptors generally define the specific package content and include product variety, flavor, features, or benefits. Descriptors may highlight new product extensions and are important to the marketing strategy. Marketers use the product descriptor to define differences among a line of products and to create visible distinctions between their product and the competition. A unique descriptor can be trademarked. Sometimes the product descriptor and the secondary copy are one and the same. Depending on the product category, descriptor copy is handled in a variety of ways, but it is always subordinate to the product name and the brand name. Usually this type is fairly basic in typographic style since it is a supporting element. If the product descriptor is the means of differentiating between product varieties and flavor, the descriptor may be designed to be part of a family look.

Romance Copy

Sometimes called the "descriptor" or "sell" copy, romance copy does what it says: it affectionately describes the personality of the product. Romance copy is the storytelling part of the text and should be positioned and designed as such. Often romance copy is smaller in size than other type on the front panel (Primary Display Panel) and is positioned independently from the brand name and product name. The product's personality and the size of the packaging often dictate the use of romance copy.

Product Descriptor

Violator

Brand Name

Sub-Brand Name

Romance Copy

Co-Branded Product

Brand Name

Sub-Brand Name

Net Wt. Statement

Graphic Device

Mandatory Copy

Throughout the world there are numerous governing bodies that oversee the labeling of consumer products. Labeling regulations exist for food, beverage, health care, over-the-counter drugs, pharmaceuticals, machinery, and many other product categories. There are recommendations for readability and mandatory requirements for specific categories.

In the United States, the Food and Drug Administration sets the guidelines for the size and positioning for all mandatory copy that must be included on packaging for food, cosmetics, drugs, and other products that are ingested or used topically. Nutrition information, ingredients, weights, measures, and product count are mandatory and regulated on food packaging in the United States. Type specifications are listed with the regulatory agency and before a packaging design goes into production, a legal authority should approve the design of the information.

Nutrition Facts

Any legible typestyle can be used, not just Helvetica. The heading "Nutrition Facts" must be the largest type size used in the nutrition label. Nutrition facts type must be larger than 8-point but does not need to be greater than 13-point. There is no specific thickness required for the three bars that separate the central sections of the nutrition

Post Cereal
Client: Kraft Foods
Design Firm:
Sterling Brands
Designer:
Sterling Studio

Elements of typography on a primary display panel.

label. The typography may be kerned as much as −4 percent, but remember that tighter kerning can reduce legibility.

Weights, Measures, and Net Quantity Statements

The net quantity of contents states the amount of product in a package. The general rule is that this copy should be no less than 3 millimeters away from the bottom (and side, if it flush right or flush left on the PDP), and no less than 3 millimeters in cap height. The typestyle should be one that is prominent and easy to read. The letters must not be more than three times as high as they are wide, and lettering must contrast sufficiently with the background to ease readability.

Ingredients Copy

Ingredients must be in a single easy-to-read, legible typeface, printed in all black or one color type on a white or other neutral contrasting background (whenever practical). The font can be either upper- and lowercase letters, except on very small packages, at least 1-point leading, and consist of letters that do not touch. (For more information see www.cfsan.fda.gov/dms/ds-label.html.)

Special provisions to labeling are given to small businesses, foods served in restaurants, food delivered to homes ready for immediate consumption, delicatessen-type food, bakery items, foods that provide no significant nutrition (coffee and most spices), fresh produce, and bulk foods with packages labeled "This unit is not for resale."

Anyone involved with designing a consumer product package should consult the specific regulatory information provided by the appropriate governing body.

GREEN & BLACK'S
ORGANIC
MILK
CHOCOLATE
WITH 34% COCOA SOLIDS FOR
A RICH CHOCOLATEY FLAVOUR
FAIRTRADE MEANS A BETTER
DEAL FOR COCOA PRODUCERS
100g ℮ NetWt 3.5oz

GREEN & BLACK'S
ORGANIC
WHITE
CHOCOLATE
REAL BOURBON VANILLA
BLENDED WITH RICH COCOA
BUTTER & FULL-CREAM MILK
FOR A RICH & SMOOTH TASTE
100g ℮ NetWt 3.5oz

GREEN & BLACK'S
ORGANIC
DARK
CHOCOLATE
MADE WITH 70% COCOA
SOLIDS FROM CACAO
ORGANICALLY GROWN IN
RAINFOREST HIGHLANDS
100g ℮ NetWt 3.5oz

DARK 70%
GREEN
&BLACK'S
ORGANIC
DARK CHOCOLATE WITH
70% COCOA SOLIDS
100g ℮

WHITE
GREEN
&BLACK'S
ORGANIC
CREAMY VANILLA
WHITE CHOCOLATE
100g ℮

MILK
GREEN
&BLACK'S
ORGANIC
A DARKER SHADE OF
MILK CHOCOLATE
100g ℮

Green & Black's Redesign
Client:
Green & Black's
Design Firm:
Pearlfisher
Art Director:
Shaun Bower

(redesign bottom)
The redesigned
PDP is simplified,
the brand identity is
modified for greater
impact, the varieties
are better defined
through hierarchy
and color, and the
spot varnish G&B
background all create
a powerful new look.

Key Points about Typography

✓ There are no straightforward answers to typographic design problems; it takes extensive experimentation to get the few appropriate and successful solutions.

✓ Time is money: do not waste time looking through hundreds of typefaces. Find a few fonts that meet the design criteria.

✓ Take a typeface and tweak it to meet the packaging design criteria and create a unique, ownable, and exclusive brand identity.

✓ Skillful typographic use is a result of proper type selection combined with design finesse, attention to kerning, spacing, ligatures, type weights, alignment, positioning, scale, composition, color, contrast, and graphic treatment.

✓ X-heights (proportion of the lowercase letter height relative to the uppercase cap height) can be sized to create greater contrast.

✓ Kerning should always be examined: the computer does not have the eye to make the spacing between letterforms perfect; this is the job of the designer.

✓ Proper spelling and grammar is critical to communication: use spell check, read copy silently and aloud, and look at every word for errors.

6 COMMUNICATING WITH COLOR

Basics of Color

Philosophers, scientists, researchers, and educators have all studied the complex activity of seeing color. Biologist Nicholas Humphrey attributes man's ability to sense color to his desire for pleasure and need for survival. "If men take pleasure in looking at a particular sight…we may expect that the consequences of their doing so—whatever they may be—are beneficial." Humphrey believes that the ability to see color (such as the glowing red of an ember) evolved to meet man's biological need for survival.

The human eye sees color before the brain recognizes imagery in the form of shapes, symbols, words, or other visual elements. Seeing color is a complex process. Objects, shapes, and images are recorded in our brains through light. Absorbed in the eye's retina, light sends a signal to the brain. The National Bureau of Standards estimates that the human eye can distinguish more than ten million different colors. Color vision and the perception of millions of colors are dependent on the mixing of different amounts of wavelengths of light.

The color system is based on color in the form of projected or reflected light. Projected light is what gives the perception of brightness, and it is this light that creates the colors' value. Reflected light is how we see color on the surface of things. An object does not emit any light of its own, but light is either absorbed or reflected off of its

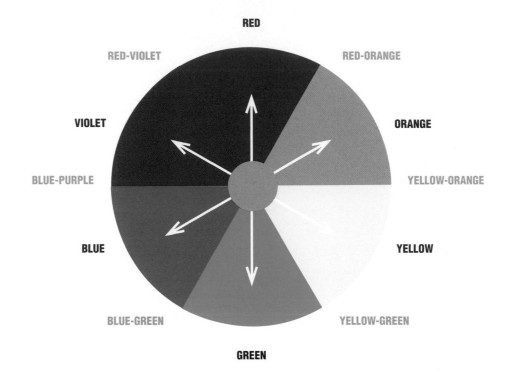

Color Wheel
The traditional color wheel is divided into three primary colors and three secondary colors. This color continuum includes all the intermediate hues produced as each one overlaps the adjacent hue. Colors opposite each other on the color wheel are complementary.

surface. Sunlight is the standard by which colors are measured. Since color in daylight changes with each different light source, natural light is as ephemeral as color itself. Painted and printed matter creates color by reflecting light off of substances such as paint, ink, dye, and toner. Color is constantly changing because light is constantly changing.

Color Terminology

Understanding color terminology helps to effectively communicate about color. The variety of a color is called *hue*—often the terms *color* and *hue* are used interchangeably—where hue is the physical attribute by which colors are distinguished from one another. On a color spectrum, colors are considered to be similar to one or a combination of two hues: red, orange, yellow, green, blue, or violet. Black, gray, and white are considered to be neutral. A *tint* is a pure color mixed with white; a *shade* is a pure color mixed with black. *Saturation* is the purity or intensity of a color. The amount of pigment in a color, defined by the strength or vividness of a hue, is saturation. The lightness or darkness of a color is its *value*. The color spectrum is defined as the image formed when light is spread out according to its wavelength by being refracted through a color prism.

Color communicates psychologically by creating a mental association. This mental association with color is what determines an individual's perception of an object or its surroundings. Although people within similar environments share general color

associations, individual reactions to color are affected by cultural backgrounds and shared social interpretations. Although color connotations change over time, for consumers from similar cultural and geographic backgrounds fundamental meanings remain consistent.

Color Distinguishes the Packaging Design

Color is one of the most influential aspects of packaging design. Consumers are more likely to identify the color of a package or product before any other visual feature. Color distinguishes a product's personality, draws attention to its attributes, and enables it to stand apart from competitors within a chaotic retail environment. Purchasing decisions are often made because of it.

Color can be used to signal the manufacturer (the red triangle of Nabisco) and the brand (the blue logo of Dove). Color can indicate culture, gender, age, ethnicity, regional locale, and price, or distinguish visual and typographic elements. Used in appropriate ways, it can break product categories and differentiate product varieties—ingredients, flavors, or fragrances—within a product line.

Jill Morton, a color consultant and the CEO of Colorcom states, "As a marketing tool, color can be a subliminally persuasive force. As a functional component of human vision, color can capture attention, relax or irritate the eyes, and contribute to the success of a product, a service, or even an interior space. The wrong colors can be a costly mistake."

Yellow Tail
Client:
Casella Wines
Design Firm:
Harkness
Walker Design
Designer:
Barbara Harkness

The distinctive kangaroo character, brand typography, and bright bold colors are visual cues that serve to help consumers find their product "flavor" or variety.

Color Associations Vary

Color connotations are both product and category specific, however an understanding of color associations is an important factor in the design process.

Red, a warm-spectrum color, is associated with the sun and heat, and can symbolize love, fire, passion, aggression, impulsiveness, excitement, daring, and power. Red can also imply danger or emergency and elicit feelings of aggression and fear. Deep rich red communicates sophistication, royalty, authenticity, seriousness, and effectiveness; while a bright red can be provocative and lively. Red can physically speed up heart rate and raise blood pressure. In packaging design, red is commonly used as an attention grabber. Red can symbolize the intensity of flavor (barbecue, spicy, hot) or the fruitiness of strawberry, raspberry, apple, or cherry. In China red symbolizes luck, prosperity, and happiness and is worn by brides. The red color used on Ritz Crackers packaging is stimulating and intense, and makes the product visually dominate the category.

Orange, similar to red, is frequently associated with the warmth of the sun, energy, exuberance, enthusiasm, adventurousness, cheerfulness, and contentment. Orange can communicate a strong and vibrant brand in one category and communicate a zesty, spicy, or fruity flavor in another. In personal-care products, orange can relate with sun and skin-care products. For Arm & Hammer Baking Soda the color orange conveys a strong, reliable brand, while the orange of Tide detergent is both attention grabbing and expresses the product's effectiveness.

Yellow symbolizes life, sun, warmth, idealism, energy, and playfulness. Yellow is a positive color and is used to suggest hope ("Tie the yellow ribbon 'round the old oak tree") but can also communicate hazard or danger. Yellow is eye stimulating—in fact, the most simulating color of the spectrum—however, when used in moderation it is the ultimate attention grabber. In the food product category yellow is often used to communicate a lemon or butter flavor, sunlight, wholesomeness, and farm freshness. In household products yellow communicates both effectiveness and caution. In some cultures yellow has the negative connotation of cowardice and deceit.

Mallomars
The yellow background creates attention-grabbing impact on shelf.

Green symbolizes down-to-earth, tranquillity, life, youth, freshness, and organic. Green communicates recycling, renewal, nature, and the environment. Green can also imply action, good luck, wealth, and money. Thought to be the easiest color on the eyes, green has a calming effect, and its use across many product categories conveys relaxation and peacefulness. On the other hand, green can represent jealousy (green with envy). In many cultures green means "go." In the use of colors for flavor descriptors on packaging design, green can represent mint, sour, apple, and lime. In recent years consumer preference for green has increased due to trends in decorating and fashion. In the competitive marketing mix, green is increasingly used in packaging designs to signal the health benefit of a product.

Bigelow, Lipton, Nescafé, and Maxwell House Decaffeinated
In the coffee and tea categories, green signals the decaffeinated varieties.

SnackWell, Healthy Choice, Friendship, and Hellmann's
Green, in the food category, has been accepted as a color that can signify a reduced-fat alternative.

Carb Smart and Carb Options
Client: Breyers/ Unilever
Design Firm: Smith Design
Designers: Carol Konkowski

Distinctive brand identity, packaging architecture, and color story for Carb Smart is Unilever's low-carbohydrate initiative in the ice-cream category. The success of the brand was quickly extended to the Carb Options umbrella brand across a range of categories, structures, and substrates with a powerful color impression.

Blue symbolizes authority, dignity, loyalty, truth, and wisdom but can also represent depression, sadness, and solitude. Blue can communicate confidence, strength, conservatism (the blue power suit of Wall Street), trust, stability, and security (police uniforms). Blue can have a peaceful, relaxing feeling (sky blue) or a sobering effect (having the "blues"). The range of colors within the blue family can shift an association from productivity and strength to calmness and relaxation. Regarded highly by both genders in Western culture, blue is used to signify the male gender in American culture, while in China blue is associated with immortality. Blue is a color not commonly found in nature and therefore has had negative connotations in food packaging design (it can indicate mold), but now it is used quite frequently. Blue can be used to counter or complement the color red. The blue color of Tylenol PM's packaging design underscores the nighttime use of the product.

Historically purple pigment was difficult to acquire through natural sources. In fact—the word *purple* comes from the snail or mollusk, *purpura*, and the coloring agent from its mucus glands—and therefore it was rare, expensive, and used primarily by wealthy nobility or high priests. Purple came to symbolize sophistication, royalty, luxury, prosperity, wisdom, spirituality, sensuality, mystery, passion, and bravery (as in the Purple Heart). In its deepest tone purple can bring about a sense of peace but also depression and darkness. For healing and health-related products, purple can signify mind, body, and spirit; and for products in the food category, purple can indicate berry flavors, such as grape and blueberry. In packaging design for youth-oriented products purple can be fresh, exotic, fun, and bold, and it falls in between two primary colors: the conservative color blue and the provocative color red.

Black can symbolize sturdiness, reliability, constancy, and wisdom, and it resonates power. In the fashion world black is bold, hip, serious, upscale, elegant, sophisticated, and luxurious, and is perceived as a classic color. Until recent years black was a clear choice for many product designs for its implication of a serious and reliable product. The use of the color black in packaging design can help to enhance other colors and make them "pop" into view. Black can create a perception of depth and communicate strength and clarity. In Western cultures, black can be the color of despair and mourning, and can be associated with evil (as in black magic).

Breyers Ice Cream
Design Firm:
Gerstman + Meyers/
Interbrand

The 1980s Gerstman + Meyers packaging design was the not only first in the ice-cream category to use black as the predominant color for the brand but reintroduced black as a color in the food category.

Smartfood and Terra Chips
Black was not a color choice for packaging design in the snack food category until Smartfood was launched in the mid-1980s. Other newfangled and nonconventional snack food products soon followed.

Lean Cuisine
(before top)

**Lean Cuisine
Redesign**
Client: Nestlé USA
Design Firm:
Wallace Church, Inc.
Creative Director:
Stan Church
Art Director:
Wendy Church
Designer:
Jhomy Irrazaba

The white
background of Lean
Cuisine presents
the food as the
hero element of the
packaging, making
a clean, uncluttered
impression in
the frozen-dinner
category.

White communicates purity, freshness, innocence, cleanliness, efficaciousness, truthfulness, and contemporariness. White can connote snow or coldness. White reflects light and makes the colors around it stand out. Until recently white was the predominant color in the medical and pharmaceutical packaging design categories, implying efficaciousness; and its association with purity made it the choice in the dairy category. In luxury packaging white can be rich and classic, but it can also be generic and nondescriptive. In Western cultures white represents purity and is the color that brides wear; however, in traditional Chinese culture it represents mourning.

Brand Building and Color

Over the years packaging design colors began to define consumer product categories. In the personal-care, health, and beauty categories the use of soft colors including pinks, purples, cool blues, greens, and neutral shades of black, gray, tan, and cream has been commonplace. The pasta aisle in the supermarket has been dominated by blue boxes and red labels for sauce jars and cans. In the cereal category packaging designs have used primary colors to grab the immediate attention of young shoppers attracted to bold colors and shapes. Red, blue, and white have been commonly used in the dairy section.

The job of drawing attention to the packaging design has been aided by developments in ink technologies. The use of neon colors, holographic overlays, and other innovative printing techniques are inventive additions to color as an attention grabber.

With the proliferation of consumer brands over the last few years, color categories have been dissolved. Many brands that once had as few as ten products in their family may now have as many as a few thousand. With this explosion of brand families comes the need for more colors to differentiate between product varieties and to distinguish products from their competitors. Additionally the marketing of consumer products across continents necessitates the need for brands to align their colors globally to make certain that colors translate the brand image consistently across a diverse consumer audience.

Similar to the design of fashion and interiors, packaging design is enhanced by coordinated color schemes. Color schemes that are complementary or contrasting, analogous or monochromatic, dominant or recessive can all help distinguish products and information. Accent colors can highlight flavor, ingredients, scent, or other product varieties and draw attention to a focal point on the packaging design.

Cambridge SilverSmiths
Client: Cambridge SilverSmiths. LTD
Design Firm: Parham Santana
Creative Director: Maruchi Santana
Senior Art Director: Maryann Mitkowski
Designer: Emily Pak

The analogous color scheme distinguishes each product variety, establishes differentiation within the product line, and sets the character for a brand that connects to women seeking style and personality in tabletop.

Heinz EZ Squirt Ketchup
Client: H.J. Heinz
Design Firm: Interbrand

The unique colors in this category were a radical departure from the consumers' perception of ketchup.

Little Monsters Hair Care
Client: Superdrug Stores Plc
Design Firm: Turner Duckworth
Creative Director: David Turner, Bruce Duckworth
Designer/ Typographer: Sam Lachian
Illustrator: Nathan Jurevicius
Account Manager: Moira Riddell

Color characterizes products marketed to a targeted consumer audience.

Redken for Men
Client: L'Oréal
Design Firm: Bergman Associates NYC
Designer: Robert Bergman

A rich background color with simple secondary color accents suggests superior value and commands a higher price.

Lamaze
Client:
Learning Curve
International, LLC
Design Firm:
Parham Santana
Creative Director:
John Parham
Senior Art Director:
Maryann Mitkowski
Designer: Emily Pak

A strategic line
extension for a
specialty infant brand.
When marketing to
children (and their
parents) in just about
any product category,
bright colors are
universal.

Owning Color in Packaging Design

Countless consumer products are recognized by the color of their packaging design. The color is a significant facet of the product's personality or brand image. When the color is "inherently distinctive" or possesses a secondary meaning (the consumer associates the packaging design as immediately identifiable as a specific brand), it can be trademarked and be part of the overall "trade dress" of the package. Size, shape, graphic configuration, color, and other nonfunctional components of the design can be trademarked.

The consistent use of a color on one packaging design or across a line of products can establish the color as an identifier of the brand. This consistency can ward off competitive products from intentionally infringing on a product's trade dress. Since packaging designs are widely identified for their colors, "ownership" of a color can help protect it through legal means (See Chapter 12: Understanding Legal Issues).

Color Forecasting and Trends

Color meanings and preferences change according to cultural trends and are forecasted like the weather. The fashion apparel and accessories, home products, and automotive products industries are trendsetters and followers of color forecasting.

Color trends derive from myriad social, political, economical, technological, and cultural influences within societies across the globe. Since color is a key determinant in consumer sales, color forecasting can be crucial. Forecasters identify specific colors for their ability to influence salability in the consumer product industries. The Color Association of the United States, the Color Marketing Group, and the Pantone Institute are among the leading forecasting entities.

In the packaging design of consumer goods, color trend awareness is an important factor in assuring that a packaging design's color is current. It is wise, however, to consider "trendy" colors from fashion or other product design areas carefully because they may be short-lived, lasting only a season or two. The human response to the color of a packaging design is affected by factors that vary from other design disciplines. The application and coordination of colors within a brand or product line must meet specific marketing objectives. Although fashion and other global color trends can be used as a guide to packaging color choice, not only does consumer behavior differ from one retail environment to another but the packaging design and product's shelf life differ greatly from the duration of a fashion item. Consumer products must stand a longer test of time. An understanding of the basic science of color, color theory, human perception of color, and consumer behavior should guide appropriate color choice.

Pantone Inc. is the world's leading authority on color. Its founder, Lawrence Herbert, developed a color-management system to specify, match, communicate, and produce accurate color. Pantone provides color formula guides, systems, and charts for the global design community. The PANTONE MATCHING SYSTEM® is a standardized color communication system that depicts thousands of precisely printed colors alongside formulas for mixing them. Used by designers and printers, the system ensures consistency since color can be specified and matched exactly.

PACKAGING DESIGN AND COLOR ASSOCIATION

Stroll through the marketplace and determine which packaging design colors best match the following characteristics:

■ Appetizing	■ Bold	■ Efficacious	■ Energetic
■ Fun	■ Original	■ Serious	■ Sophisticated
■ Strong	■ Trendy	■ Urban	■ Youthful

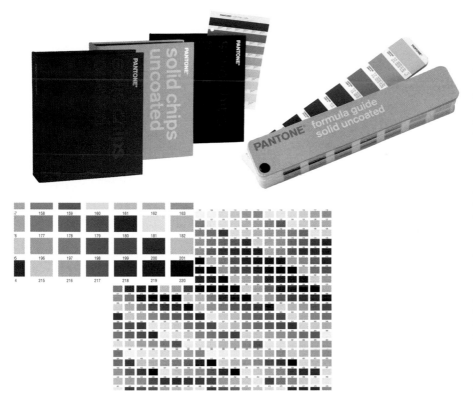

PANTONE MATCHING SYSTEM®
Fan and Swatch Books
PANTONE® and other Pantone, Inc. trademarks are the property of Pantone, Inc.

PANTONE® software addresses color issues in the digital world and bridges design and production through color technology.

Color Sheet
Since color printed from a desktop printer will not print exactly the same way as a high end professional printer, it is necessary to compare color swatches. Creating a test page for the assigned PANTONE® colors will show how they reproduce from a specific printer.

Color on the Computer Screen

Matching what is visible on the computer screen and the printed color is always a challenge. Not only do colors vary between computer screens, but also they vary for different materials, substrates, and objects. Every colored object and printed surface absorbs and reflects light, whereas computer screens transmit light—therefore color is seen differently.

Although manufacturers of computer monitors, peripherals, and software continuously work to ensure color accuracy and consistency throughout the design process, the colors on a computer screen and the colors on printed objects have different properties. "What you see is what you get" is a term that resonates true in the client presentation process. The color on a design concept that has been presented and approved by the client is exactly what the client expects to see in the final produced packaging design. With constantly evolving technologies, processes, and materials in packaging design, the consistent use, application, and production of matching colors continues to be a significant challenge. Constant color adjustment and alignment is a necessary part of the design process since it is essential that from initial concept to final printed packaging design colors be uniform and consistent.

Packaging Design and Color in Retail

An understanding of how a packaging design's color is impacted by the retail environments in which the product will exist is essential. The color of a packaging design can be affected by the store's interior lighting. Ceiling height, aisle lighting, quality of light (dim, bright, or dark), the use of fluorescent, incandescent, or colored lights all impact the consumer's perception of the color. Packaging designs should be evaluated in their retail environment to assure color accuracy.

BREAKING THROUGH THE SHELF CLUTTER

Color has a direct impact on each brand's "shelf impact," including its visibility and shop-ability. In terms of visibility, *PRS Eye-Tracking* studies have consistently shown that "brand blocking" (through the consistent use of color) improves shelf impact. This fact applies to both visibility (the likelihood of being actively considered) and speed of noting (the likelihood of visually pre-empting competition at the shelf).

However, contrary to popular belief, no single color is inherently "more visible" at retail than any other color. That's because visibility is a function of color contrast: For example, Tylenol's bright red packaging should "break through clutter" if positioned next to Advil's blue, but it might well "blend right in" and become recessive if positioned next to Motrin's bright orange (or store brand packaging that copies its color scheme). In other words, the "right" color for shelf impact is also situational.

To make things even more complicated, the color consistency that enhances a brand's shelf visibility can detract from its variety differentiation and shop-ability. Without question, people do "shop by color" (i.e. *"I look for the yellow bag"*) and color-coding is the most effective way to differentiate flavors or varieties.

Scott Young, President
Perception Research Services, Inc.

Key Points about Color

✓ Consider color as it communicates the design's personality.

✓ Apply colors across product lines in a coordinated color scheme and across the packaging structures, materials, and substrates of a brand.

✓ Match color from the computer to the specified color for the final printed material.

7 COMMUNICATING WITH IMAGERY

Imagery and Cultural Perception

The perception of imagery differs from culture to culture. Unlike color, images have fewer standard interpretations and represent different things to different people. In American culture a daisy is a flower that visually communicates springtime, freshness, vitality, and love (picking flower petals to "Does she love me or does she not"), whereas in France this flower communicates mourning, sorrow, and sadness. The visual image of the bottom of a character's shoe is considered rude in many Asian cultures, while in Western cultures it has little significance. The hand symbol for victory in the United States is an insult when turned around in Europe.

Effective Uses of Imagery

When used effectively on packaging design, imagery—whether illustrative or photographic—can make a strong visual impression. Its use can be unexpected or unanticipated and can heighten consumer interest. Consumers look at pictures before they read text. When used appropriately images are effective design tools ("A picture is worth a thousand words").

Illustrations, photographs, icons, symbols, and characters can be executed in a multitude of styles that each create a rich visual language and provide visual stimuli. Imagery can be simple, offering the quick recognition of a concept, or it can be complex or subliminal, taking the viewer much more than a moment or two to fully comprehend the meaning. Consider the sensory experiences that different visuals communicate: flavor, scent, taste, and temperature (including the sensation of a spicy food) can all be communicated visually in packaging design.

Imagery is dependent upon its directness and appropriateness in communicating the brand personality and specific product attributes. The communication of appetite appeal on a food packaging design, the connotation of lifestyle, the suggestion of mood, and instruction of product use are all ways imagery shapes packaging design.

Extensive creative exploration that focuses on the strategic objectives outlined by the client will narrow the choice of the appropriate imagery needed to effectively support a concept. A marketing brief that is written in a descriptive way can create a visual picture of what the client ultimately wants to achieve.

LIQUID IMAGERY

The appropriate use of visual imagery is the key to the successful communication of a product or brand personality. Liquid imagery can be challenging to execute because of its visceral qualities. There are both illustrative and photographic styles that can successfully communicate the characteristics of liquids.

Liquid imagery can convey comforting or refreshing and quenching qualities such as warm and steamy or cold and frosty. The imagery can be depicted splashing and pouring, bubbly and effervescent, or sweating with condensation. Liquid can be water running in a stream, cascading down a waterfall, or pouring from a pitcher. There are equally as many execution styles, ranging from close-up photographs of liquid to watercolor renderings. The possibilities are endless. Each choice of imagery provides a distinct visual way to communicate a message or personality.

Acuvue
Client:
Johnson &
Johnson
Vision Care
Design Firm:
Colemanbrandworx
(CBX)
Designers:
Jim Williams,
Allison Koller

For contact lens wearers this liquid image serves to visually communicate a product that does not dry out.

THE TOUCHPOINT IN PACKAGING DESIGN

Images can create visual excitement, memorable experiences, and recognizable "touchpoints". Touchpoint is a marketing term used in packaging design that refers to the one critical visual element that strategically connects the brand to the consumer and becomes what the consumer visually identifies with the product.

Pringles
The Pringles character, with his handlebar mustache and dapper bow tie, boosts consumers' recognition with the Pringles brand and its packaging design.

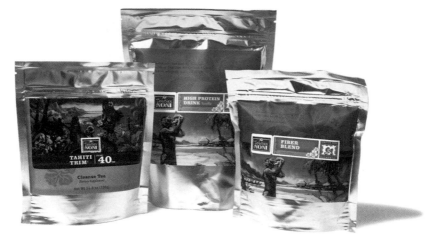

Invigor8
Client: Campbell
Soup Company
Design Firm:
Sterling Brands
Designer:
Sterling Studio

Tahitian Noni
Client: Tahitian Noni
Design Firm:
Hornall Anderson
Design Works
Designers:
Jack Anderson,
Lisa Cervany,
James Tee,
Tiffany Place,
Leo Raymundo,
Jana Nishi,
Elmer dela Cruz,
Bruce Branson-
Meyer

Island Nuts
Client: Island Nuts
Design Firm:
Sterling Brands
Designer:
Sterling Studio

Illustration and Photography as Mediums for Imagery

As there are hundreds of illustration styles, ranging from simple line drawings to elaborate paintings, each specific style can be used to convey a brand's distinct personality. There are an equal number of photographic styles and ways an image can be colored or rendered. Photographic images can be in black-and-white or one color, duotones, tints, screens, or in full color. When combined with printed words, images expand the meaning and interpretation of the overall design. With today's technology photographic images are often combined with illustrations to create unique effects.

Elsa's Story
The contrast between the black-and-white photograph and the "hero" photo of the product brilliantly evokes both nostalgia and appetite appeal, giving this gourmet line of cookies, crackers, and gift collections a distinctive personality.

**Rubbermaid
Elegan**

Client: Newell
Rubbermaid
Design Firm:
Parham Santana
Creative Director:
John Parham
Designer: Emily Pak

Photography is clean
and simply styled for
the presentation of
functional products
in housewares.

**Brita Product
Photography**

Client: Brita
Design Firm:
Hornall Anderson
Design Works
Designers:
Jack Anderson,
James Tee,
Andrew Wicklund,
Gretchen Cook,
Andrew Smith,
Jay Hilburn,
Michael Brugman,
John Anderle

Considerations for
product depiction,
include the
perspective or angle
of the lens, lighting
and styling, and
the cropping and
positioning of the
product.

Imagery can be used in packaging designs to:

- show the product;
- depict the target consumer;
- set a mood (landscape, flower, scene);
- provide credibility (celebrity image);
- appeal to the appetite.

Appetite Appeal

Appetite-appeal illustration or photography can present the "serving suggestion"—the prepared product styled with the appropriate dishes, serving utensils, and props that set the tone and provide enticement. This type of imagery not only educates the consumer on etiquette and proper presentation but also attracts attention by being distinctive on the shelf, looking savory, and figuratively whetting their appetites. Shoppers are constantly looking for convenient meal solutions and appetizing images that appeal to their senses.

"Hero" beauty shots or luscious illustrations of food products grab the consumers' attention, are the focal point on the package and effectively give a brand shelf impact to stand out from its competition.

Organic Valley Soy
Client: Organic Valley Family of Farms
Design Firm: Webb Scarlett deVlam
Creative Director: Richard Barkaway
Brand Strategy: Ronald de Vlam
Designer: Webb Scarlett deVlam team

The combined use of illustration and photography sets the scene and creates appetite appeal.

Home Safe
Client: Helix
Design Firm:
Toast
Designers:
Vicky Arzano,
Lori Yi Golden

The design of
the imagery is an
important factor in
setting the tone for
the product.

Cropping and Scaling Images

Imagery must be designed to fit within the context of the layout, not the other way around. Cropping and scaling an image can provide endless ways to incorporate it into a design. Positioning a frame or mask over the image enables it to be examined independently from its context. This method can help identify what aspects of the image serve the overall communication objectives of the design. Extraneous parts of an image should be eliminated if they do not add impact to the design concept. The visual communication should be clear, direct, and immediately understood by the consumer.

Instructional Illustration

Instructional illustration is defined as imagery that is informative, functional, or educational. This type of visual is generally used in packaging design to depict a "how to" process. These illustrations stand apart from the more aesthetic visual elements and serve an important purpose in providing direction for the consumer.

Instructional illustrations can be used to visually depict:

- How to open the packaging
- How to close or reseal the packaging
- How to use or prepare the product
- Precautionary warnings or hazards

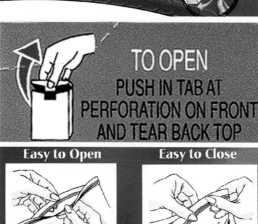

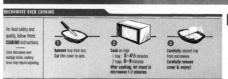

Instructional Illustrations
Whether the illustration communicates a tamper-proof packaging design or the method of storage or disposal, instructional images can be executed in a simple line-art illustration style that details the visual communication objectives.

Characters

Characters can be developed to support brand communication, promote product attributes, and become the embodiment of the brand's personality. Since the possible qualities, traits, and features of these characters are infinite, creating just the right one to communicate the personality of the brand can be a daunting challenge.

Ethnic connotations, gender, facial expressions, body type, skin color, shape, size, graphic layout, and design styles—whether expressed photographically or illustratively—all affect the communication. A character can have a human or animal form, be depicted illustratively or photographically, or have a cartoon style with no human likeness. Characters can have universal appeal to kids and adults alike, and can break through cultural barriers. The gesture of a character can communicate emotional attributes such as confidence, strength, trust, happiness, energy, and amusement. Characters should be charismatic, engaging, and appealing. The depiction of these qualities can captivate consumers, stimulate sales, and create brand identification. Brand confidence and loyalty can be tied into the image of a character because ultimately consumers want to trust and relate to the "look" of the brand's personality.

Brawny Man Character Evolution
1970s (left),
Late 1990s (middle),
2003 (right)

When there is a strong consumer connection to the character, the character alone can symbolize the brand without other supporting visual elements, and can become a cultural icon—almost a brand unto itself.
Used with permission of Georgia-Pacific Corporation, Atlanta GA.

Characters Grid
These characters have evolved through the years to appear fresh and new and to reflect the current society's values on gender, aging, stereotypes, and race:
Mr. Clean®, Morton Salt Girl®, Paul Newman, Aunt Jemima®, Morris the Cat®, Rice Krispie® Kids, Green Giant®, Gerber Baby®, Land O'Lakes Indian Maiden®, Tony the Tiger®, Charlie the Tuna®, Quaker Oats Man®, Little Debbie®, Snuggle Bear®, and Pillsbury Doughboy®

Rice Krispies

Client: Kellogg's
Design Firm:
Smith Design
Designer:
Carol Konkowski

Kellogg's Rice
Krispie Treats
Snap, Krackle,
and Pop reached
"icon"status by being
linked direclty with
the brand name. This
dynamic redesign
speaks to consumers
in various age ranges
with it's bold and
contemporary update.

**Heart Attack
in a Bag**

Designer:
Rebecca Reiter
FIT (Fashion Institute
of Technology)

The color-coded pig
character is the brand
icon and helps to
differenciate flavor
varieties for these
pork rind snacks.

Graphic Devices

Basic design elements such as line, shape, color, texture, and type provide endless design possibilities. The creation of specific graphic devices can aid in the organization of visual information on a packaging design. Graphic elements can be used to lead the consumer through the packaging design by visually directing the eye to "read" the hierarchy of information. Graphic devices can be used individually or in combination with other devices. When well designed these devices can be used to support the organization of the layout and provide for clearer, more immediate communication.

Olay Quench
Client:
Procter & Gamble
Design Firms:
Webb Scarlett
deVlam (structural
packaging design);
LPK (graphic design)

Quench is Olay's first foray into hand and body lotions, and the outstanding holistic design set the line up for overnight success. The simple but unusual package shape makes the consumer stop and take notice.

Symbols and Icons

Symbols and icons can be simple graphic diagrams or elaborate layouts. In the development of symbols and icons for packaging design it is important to discern contradictory cultural meanings. For example, a packaging design that incorporates a distinct religious or cultural symbol without understanding its communication may be deemed offensive. The choice and design of symbols for packaging designs must be thoroughly researched and tested to ensure that they communicate what is intended.

Suzi Wan

The pattern on this packaging design unintentionally suggested the symbol recognized as a swastika, which has negative associations because of its use as the official emblem of Nazi Germany. With a redesign, the pattern was modified.

Amazon.com Box
Client: Amazon.com
Design Firm: Turner Duckworth
Creative Directors: David Turner, Bruce Duckworth
Designer: Antony Biles
Account Manager: Joanne Chan

In a market where most competitors were using plain brown boxes, a big smile was put on the Amazon.com box as a way of making a million good impressions a week without spending any extra money.

Tag Body Spray
(above)

Axe Deodorant Body Spray
The explosive symbols reflect the design style of gaming graphics familiar to the young male consumer.

Violators

Violator is the term used for the visual device that is generally positioned on top of packaging graphics and is used for the purpose of calling attention to or announcing a special feature of the product or package. These devices purposefully disturb—violate—the design of the PDP. Violators are frequently used to communicate federally regulated product claims, announce size, quantity, quality, and bring attention to new features.

Common Violators for Food Product Claims

- Fat Free/Wheat Free/Dairy Free/Sodium Free
- Cholesterol Free/Reduced Fat/Low Calorie
- Light/Fresh/Unsweetened/Unsalted
- Low Fat/Extra Lean
- Good Source of (Dietary Fiber, Vitamins)

New Violators
Violators are commonplace on packaging designs in the supermarket and are often used to communicate product claims, changes in packaging materials, functions such as resealable packages, or a new size for easier storage.

Graphic Devices on packaging designs can include:

- color bars for product variety, color, scent, flavor, ingredients, or fragrance;
- violators to communicate new products, product benefits, packaging benefits, or price;
- arrows and shapes to direct the eye, add energy, or contain text;
- squares, circles, triangles, and rectangles to separate a body of copy or enclose a brand identity;
- texture as background for aesthetics or to support photos, illustrations, or symbols.

Exploring design strategy through an array of imagery styles and colors is crucial. There is more than one way to visualize an image and execute an idea. Images should be researched extensively and refined through narrowing down appropriate illustrative and photographic styles. This process should take into account different ways of cropping, rendering, and coloring an image, and is an important step toward making certain that each image chosen not only matches the product's personality but also communicates across a diverse consumer market.

Key Points about Imagery

✓ The perception of imagery differs from culture to culture.

✓ "A picture is worth a thousand words."

✓ Illustrations, photographs, icons, symbols, and characters can be executed in a multitude of styles that each create a rich visual language and provide visual stimuli.

✓ Imagery is dependent upon its directness and appropriateness in communicating the brand personality and specific product attributes.

✓ Exploring design strategy through an array of imagery styles and colors is crucial.

✓ A touchpoint becomes what the consumer visually identifies with the product.

✓ Imagery must be designed to fit within the context of the layout, not the other way around.

8 STRUCTURES AND MATERIALS

Structure and Materials in Packaging Design

In the consumer's mind, the package is the product. For many products, the physical configuration embodies the brand's visual identity. The structure and materials serve as containment, protection, and transportation of the product and provide the physical surface on which the packaging design exists.

In the retail environment the packaging structure supports the product's shelf life and presence and provides tactile qualities and protective features that all affect the product's initial consumer appeal. The structure ultimately resides in the hands of the end user, where it performs ergonomic tasks including opening and closing properly, dispensing, and in some cases safely storing the product. Consideration of the materials and their advantages and disadvantages must be taken into consideration at the onset of every packaging design assignment.

Packaging structure and choice of material are based on the following considerations:

- What is the product?
- How will the product be transported?
- How and where will the product be stored?
- How does the product need to be protected?

■ How will the product be displayed?

■ Where will the product be sold?

■ Who is the target consumer?

■ What is the category competition?

■ What are the cost constraints?

■ What are the production quantities?

■ What is the production timetable?

■ Can a pre-existing structure be reengineered?

■ Can a new structure be selected from a stock source?

■ Does a new structure need to be developed?

■ Should the structure be proprietary?

Structural and material decisions can be the most critical issues since they lead to the effective protection and transportation of the product, and ultimately consumer satisfaction. The structure and materials may be dictated by what is readily available in the market or by new technology and innovations. Whatever the case, the foundation for the packaging design is determined by structural design factors.

Kellogg's Drink and Crunch
Manufacturers have introduced new structures and materials for cereal packaging to address single-serve applications, portability, and convenience.

Pepperidge Farms Whims
An innovative paperboard structure for an established brand provides a new means of portability and resealability.

Explorations of Cereal Packaging Design
Designers:
LiMei Chen (left),
Min Jung Choi/ FIT
(Fashion Institute of
Technology)

These design explorations focused on convenience and portability with single-serve applications. The development of new unique, eye-appealing structures provided the option of on-the-go use.

"GETTING OUT OF THE BOX"

In demonstrating how structure and material can change what is characteristic about a category, a student project explored the cereal aisle in the supermarket with the objective to "get out of the box." Consideration included convenience (product delivery, resealability, portability, and single-serve use) and added value through interactive product use. (*Added value* is a term for a product's packaging design that provides benefits above and beyond what is expected.)

In the United States cereal products are generally packaged in large paperboard cartons. These structures provide an expansive amount of packaging real estate, which clamors for brand recognition. Even with all the brand elements, there is plenty of room for on-pack promotions, back-panel offers, puzzles, and activities that keep the box in front of the consumer during breakfast. The paperboard structure is considered a "friendly" package because it is easily flattened for disposal, is recyclable, and is relatively cost-effective to produce. Even with consumer complaints (the biggest among consumers about typical bag-in-the-box packaging is that the bags are hard to tear open, not resealable, and a waste of space and material), finding a competitive alternative to the paperboard carton is a challenge.

A basic knowledge of the different types of materials and structures appropriate to packaging design is essential. Structure and materials can be divided into a few general categories.

Paperboard

Paperboard can be functional, cost-effective, and recyclable. Functional properties allow for structural creativity and even a simple folding carton can be a great solution since its broad, flat surfaces serve as a place to create a billboard for the brand identity.

Paperboard is the general term in the paper industry for sheets made from either virgin wood fiber or recycled paper stock. The weight of paper material is measured by the layer, ply, or by thickness in thousandths of an inch using a caliper gauge. Paperboard is differentiated from paper based on its caliper. Material less than .010 inches thick is considered paper; anything thicker than that is considered paperboard. Typically paperboard is manufactured in calipers between .010 and .040 inch, and is also referred to in points (.010 = 10 points, .040 = 40 points).

The weight or caliper of the paperboard is specific to the size and function of the carton and the containment needs of a product. The product's size and weight determines the structure and strength. The structural design is also dependent on marketing objectives of how to feature the brand and the product. The packaging may function to accommodate and protect a secondary package inside, such as a tube or bottle, or an inner structure such as a plastic tray or corrugated sleeve.

Paperboard is manufactured by laminating several layers of paper together and comes in two basic types, depending on how it is produced. Fourdrinier paperboard is made of one to four plies of mostly virgin fiber. Cylinder paperboard is made of seven to nine plies or layers from mostly recycled grades of paper fiber. There are a variety of weights and finishes of both.

The most common paperboards are:

- **SBS (solid bleached sulfate)** is made with the highest percentage of bleached virgin fiber. The most expensive paperboard, it is usually coated with clay for a premium solid white printing surface and is used primarily for packaging food, dairy, cosmetics, medicinal and pharmaceutical products.

- **SUS (solid unbleached sulfate)** is made with the highest percentage of unbleached virgin fiber. This natural Kraft paperboard is available in uncoated and coated surfaces. The strength of this material makes it a common choice for beverage carriers, hardware products, and office supplies.

- **Recycled** is a multi-ply material made from 100 percent recovered or recycled papers and paperboard, and is available in uncoated and coated sheets. Uncoated board is used for composite cans (spiral wound cylinders) and fiber drums. Coated board is used for dry food packaging including cookies, and cake mixes as well as other household goods such as paper products and powdered detergents.

- **Plain chipboard** (shirt board) is made from wastepaper and is usually gray or tan in color. It may be used for set-up boxes (generally rigid structures covered in decorative papers or other materials commonly used for gift items such as perfumes and glassware). This material is also used for other folding cartons, backing boards for blister packaging, low-end packaging, and for the inner structures not visible on the shelf. Usually plain chipboard is unsuitable for direct printing.

Corrugated Paperboard

Corrugated or containerboard is composed of paperboard with fluted "medium" paper laminated to it. One-sided is called "single-faced"; double-sided or double-faced is called "single-walled," with the fluted paper in the middle. Unlined—just the fluted paper—is often used as packing material for fragile products and objects, and as product support for inner structural packaging. The single-, double-, or triple-walled corrugated is commonly used for outer packaging such as shipping cartons and containers. Single-faced corrugated with smaller-size fluting faced on the outside is used in higher-end packaging designs for its textured look. Printed paperboard can be laminated to corrugated board for the primary packaging of heavier products: appliances, cookware, electrics/housewares (irons, toasters, dishes, glassware, etc.), and electronics (computers, cameras, etc.).

Various Examples of Corrugation
The Wiley Encyclopedia of Packaging Technology. Aaron Brody and Kenneth S. Marsh. 1997. John Wiley & Sons, Inc. Used by permission of John Wiley & Sons, Inc.

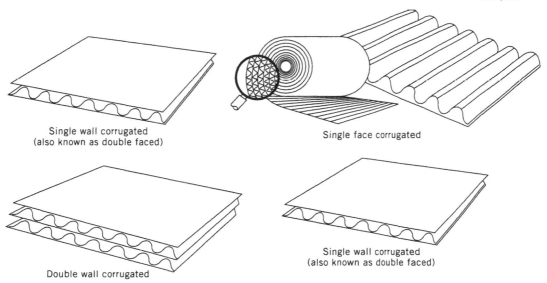

Single wall corrugated
(also known as double faced)

Single face corrugated

Double wall corrugated

Single wall corrugated
(also known as double faced)

Folding Cartons

Folding cartons are typically designed to be a one-piece construction stamped out of paperboard or corrugated paperboard, scored (creased to be folded), folded, and tabbed or glued to make a structure. The pattern or die-line of the carton includes the outside contour of its shape and all the cut and score lines that define each of its panels and their respective glue flaps to keep the carton together. It may include other details of inner die-cuts or partial cuts that add to the function of the carton.

Folding Carton Styles

The two most common styles of folding cartons are:

Reverse tuck: The top and bottom flaps alternate so that the top flap opens from front to back while the bottom flap opens back to front. The hard edge of the top of the reverse tuck should be in the back.

Straight tuck: Both the top and the bottom flaps go in the same direction. These flaps usually open back to front.

The two common folding carton closures are:

Slit locks: The tucks are slit into the top dust flaps.

Friction lock: The tucks are held in place by friction, usually on the side of the top and bottom flaps.

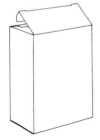

Reverse Tuck Carton
(above)

Folding Carton Die
The Packaging Designer's Book of Patterns.
George L. Wybenga and László Roth.
2003. John Wiley & Sons, Inc.
Used by permission of John Wiley & Sons, Inc.

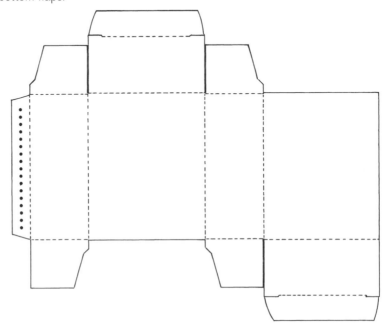

Set-Up Boxes

Set-up boxes are rigid preassembled structures with a top and bottom. They are commonly made from heavyweight paperboard or chipboard and laminated with decorative papers, material, and other finishes that cover all of the outer sides and edges. Frequently used for cosmetics, candy, jewelry, and other high-end products, these are often elaborate structures that can give the impression of luxury and add visual appeal to a product. The decorative look of set-up boxes can provide "added value" in that they are often saved for after-product reuse. New manufacturing techniques have afforded one-piece and two-piece folding cartons to be introduced with neatly rolled edges to give the appearance of a set-up box at a fraction of the cost.

Rigid Set-Up Boxes
These structures are often used for candy, cosmetics, and jewelry

Canisters

Paperboard canisters are spiral-wound in a cylinder and are manufactured in varying weights and lengths. The inner cylinder of a roll of toilet paper or paper towels is an example of a lightweight paperboard canister. Low-end canisters are usually plain paperboard while high-end canisters are used frequently as premium structures for cosmetics, lingerie, fashion accessories, and luxury products as well as for food and liquor gift boxes. Canisters can also be produced in multiple layers with protective plastic, metal film, or foil barrier layers and are commonly used as packaging structures for snacks, oatmeal, frozen juice concentrates, and refrigerated dough. In an effort to remain competitive, canister manufacturers are finding innovative ways to make their packaging structures more unique with different shapes such as ovals and asymmetrical forms, new die-cutting capabilities, and new finishing techniques.

Other Paper and Paperboard Structures

Trays, sleeves, pouches, and bags are other structures used for primary packaging designs, for inner packaging structures, or in combination for complete packaging design systems. Sleeves can take on a number of different configurations and can be die-cut in contours and shapes for distinctive appearances. Paper or lightweight paperboard is used for flexible pouches and bags. The humble square-bottomed paper bag that has been around for two centuries is still widely used for many products. As secondary packaging the paper shopping bag offers a great billboard opportunity as means for advertising a store, brand, or product. Paper bags and pouches can be lined with plastic film or foil laminate to protect the product contents.

The flexibility of paperboard as a material has provided opportunities for exciting new forms. It can be molded and formed into a variety of packaging design shapes or combined with other materials to offer a wider array of possibilities. This material provides a number of options in converting and printing finishes that create distinctive packaging designs solutions. The physical surface of paperboard prints beautifully; and when treated with embossing, foil stamping, foil laminates, matte and gloss varnishes, pearlescent coatings, and other techniques paperboard can add significantly to the look of a packaging design.

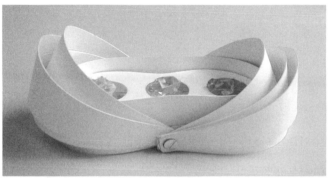

Paperboard Canister Student Competition
Designers:
Gina Taha
(top and middle),
Jana Frankova
(bottom left),
Tia Romano
(bottom right), /FIT
(Fashion Institute of
Technology)

Robinson Paperboard
Packaging,
manufacturers
of spiral-wound
canisters, sponsored
a student competition
to explore innovative
packaging structures.

Plastics

There are wide array of plastics that offer diverse qualities and properties that serve a range of containment needs. They can be rigid or flexible, clear, white or colored, transparent or opaque and can be molded into many different shapes and sizes. Thermoformed plastics are softened by heat and shaped by molding, extrusion, or pressing (calendering).

The most common types of plastics used for packaging are as follows:

Low-density polyethylene (LDPE) is used for containers and bags for clothing and food, in the form of shrink- and stretch-wrap films.

High-density polyethylene (HDPE) is rigid and opaque and is used for milk, laundry detergent, household cleaning fluids, personal-care products, and cosmetics bottles.

Poly ethylene terephthalate (PET) is clear like glass and is used for water and carbonated beverages; foods like mustard, peanut butter, edible oils, and syrups; pouches for foods and medical products.

Polypropylene is used for bottles, caps, and moisture-proof wrappings.

Polystyrene (PS) is produced in different forms. Crystal polystyrene is used to make jewel cases for CDs and bottles for pills. High-impact polystyrene is used to make thermoformed containers for dairy products. Foamed polystyrene is used for cups and clamshell containers for food (hamburgers), meat trays, and egg cartons.

Alterna Hair Care Line On Shelf
A marked difference in packaging design structure can reflect variety or line extensions within a family of product.

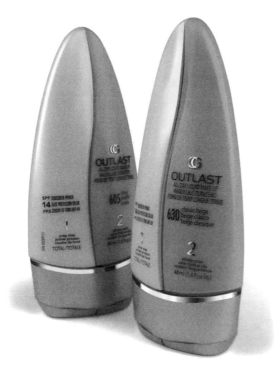

Plastic materials and manufacturing processes offer the structural designer opportunities to create innovative forms. Bottle and other structural shapes can include in-mold labeling, color options, special metallic coloring and effects, embossing, and finishing techniques such as silk-screen printing and hot stamping with foils.

Rigid plastic structures maintain their shape while holding a product. Bottles, jars, tubes, and tub-shaped forms are available as stock packaging in a multitude of contours and sizes, and can be custom made. Plastic packaging structures are used in most product categories, including milk jugs, soda bottles, butter tubs, microwavable bowls of pasta and rice, shampoo, body lotion, cold medicines, detergents, and dish soap. Plastic packaging designs with proprietary contours or shapes are easily identifiable and set the character for a product category.

Plastic tubes are filled and capped for closure with a flip top or threaded screw cap turned upside down with the cap on the bottom. Innovations in new plastic manufacturing, plastic materials, and processing methods have provided opportunities for structural designers to develop new tube shapes with contoured ends. With their tapered shape and limited display area for branding and product information, the application of graphics to tubes can be challenging. Tubes can be printed before or after they are formed. The complexity of design is limited by their respective production and printing processes. Additional structures include folding cartons, trays, and sleeves.

CoverGirl Outlast
Client:
Procter & Gamble
Design Firm:
Webb Scarlett
deVlam (structural
design); Badger and
Partners (graphic
design)

The product
demanded a
packaging design
that signaled the new
product benefits and
application method
without intimidating
or alienating the
consumer with an
overly technical
look. This goal was
achieved with dual
squeezable chambers
that travel together
and are applied
independently.

CASE STUDY

Group 4's design for Ready to Roll™, the new package for Sherwin-Williams Dutch Boy Paint, is the next generation of the paint "can." Consumer benefits include an easy-open, resealable, airtight package with a comfortable grip handle, and retailers like that it facilitates easy stacking and storage for more merchandising opportunities. Group 4 followed the same design process for proprietary structural development described in Chapter 10, beginning with research and design stimulus of how consumers use existing products. Initial concept sketches of innovative possibilities are reviewed in a brainstorming session with the design team. Black-and-white concept development continued with concept screening of 3-D rendered models and drawings.

A preferred design concept was validated with performance testing of models. The final design was executed—"the package is the product" and the design adds value and makes painting palatable.

Sherwin-Williams Structural Designs
(spread)
Client:
Sherwin-Williams
Vice President
of Marketing
Consumer
Division:
Adam Chafe
Design Firm:
Group4
Director
of Product
Research:
Bob Bruno

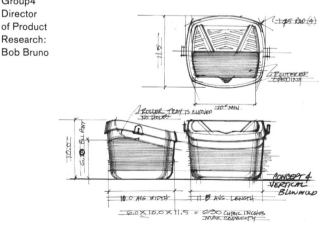

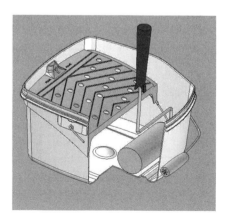

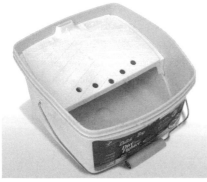

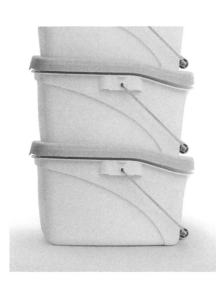

Blister Packs

Another type of rigid plastic packaging structure is the blister pack. This structure is thermoformed around the front face of a product, allowing it to be viewed through the transparent plastic. The blister is often adhered onto a paperboard backing card and is printed with packaging design graphics. Hinged or double blisters (clamshell) are formed around both sides of the product, allowing for complete product visibility. Graphics can also be printed directly on the plastic structure.

Typically blister structures are hole-punched to enable them to be pegged on a retail display. Toys, mass-merchandised cosmetics and personal-care products, over-the-counter drugs, batteries, electronics, and hardware such as nails, screws, and other small items are good examples of products sold in blister packs.

In the past, the ease with which blister packs were opened increased the risk of product pilferage. New blister designs have become considerably more difficult to open (to the dismay of consumers), but offer greater protection from shoplifting.

**Discovery
Channel Store**
Client:
Discovery Channel
Design Firm:
Parham Santana
Creative Director:
John Parham
Senior Art Director:
Dave Wang
Designer: Emily Pak

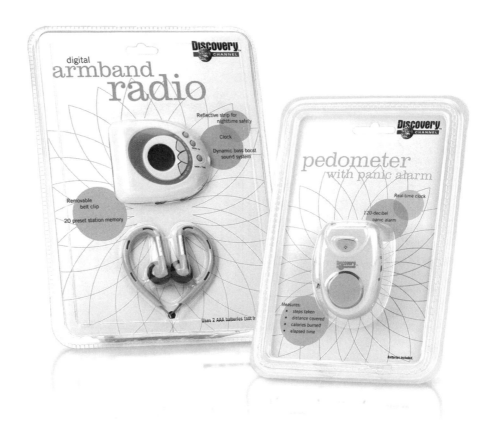

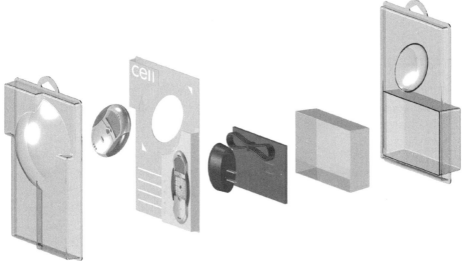

**Cell Phone
Blister Packaging**
Design Firm: Carson
Ahlman Design
Industrial Designer:
Carson Ahlman

An exploded view
of blister packaging
components.

Glass

Glass containers come in myriad shapes, sizes, and colors and are common structures in most consumer product categories. Glass can be molded into distinctive shapes with varying opening sizes and embossments, and other embellishments can enhance the overall packaging design. Innovative bottle designs using different labeling and printing techniques are a means of achieving a proprietary packaging design. The inert nature of glass (meaning it does not react with the substances it contains) makes it suitable over other materials that are prone to interact and affect certain food, drug, and other variable products.

Similarly to paperboard, glass competes with plastic as a packaging design material. The weight of glass and the ease of breakage can affect the manufacturing and shipping expenses and thus both the cost-effectiveness and the suitability of this material. With its visual and tactile qualities, glass communicates a reliable and distinctive quality material. It is the preferred packaging material for perfumes, cosmetics, pharmaceuticals, many beverages, and other gourmet food and luxury products.

With a common perception that products look, smell, and taste better in glass packaging, many alcoholic and noncarbonated beverages such as energy and sports drinks, teas, juices, and even bottled waters are packaged in glass containers (although high-quality plastic bottle are now competing with glass).

Bottle Sketches for Avon's Extraordinary/ Second Skin
Client: Avon Products
Design Firm: Avon inhouse design group
Designer: Eric Lee

In "A Touch of Glass" Andrew Kaplan states, "Over the past decade, packaging has assumed a tremendous amount of responsibility in 'advertising' products. Consumer product goods (CPG) companies like Anheuser-Busch, Coca-Cola, Del Monte, Estée Lauder, and Bacardi have increased both creative and manufacturing efforts to promote the package as the number-one marketing vehicle to sell their products. This responsibility shift has helped to promote the use of glass as a container substrate because of the inherent premium presence and supreme product protection attributes."

Absolut Bottle
Under permission of V&S Vin & Spirit AB (publ). ABSOLUT® VODKA. Absolut Country of Sweden Vodka & Logo, Absolut, Absolute Bottle Design and Absolut calligraphy are trademarks owned by V&S Vin Spirit AB (publ) ©2005 V&S Vin & Spirit AB (publ).

The design broke the mold of traditional bottle shapes in the spirits category—the neck was too short, the shoulders were too broad, and it had too much copy applied via ceramic labeling, which did away with a paper label, showing more of the product. The bottle defined the brand: "Clarity, Simplicity and Perfection." It has become a cultural icon, being the centerpiece in more than a thousand ads since.

Perfume Bottles
Proprietary glass bottle designs define the personality of these fragrances.

Metal

Metal packaging is made from tin, aluminum, and steel. The wide availability of the raw materials used to manufacture metal has made this packaging material a low-cost structure to produce. Processed foods, aerosols, paint, chemicals, and automotive products are among the common consumer products that utilize steel cans and bottles. Aluminum is frequently used in the carbonated beverage and health and beauty categories; aluminum-foil containers are used for bakery goods, meat products, and prepared foods.

Beer Bottle Can
Distinctive contours can raise the perception of the "can" as a high-end packaging design structure.

Cans

Metal cans have been around since the early 1800s, developed to supply food to the British military and then introduced in the United States, initiating the first tin-plated or coated iron can. Today metal cans are lightweight and often coated with materials that prevent product interaction. Cans are produced in either two-piece or three-piece designs. Two-piece cans are molded with a bottom and cylindrical walls, and the top is assembled separately. These cans do not have a side seam, therefore it is easier to print around the entire cylindrical surface. Carbonated beverage cans are a good example of a printed two-piece can. Three-piece cans are cylinder structures with both a top and a bottom assembled separately. Typical three-piece cans have paper labels to display brand identity and product information, such as in canned vegetables and soups. Some three-piece cans have packaging graphics printed directly on the surface. Three-piece cans are airtight and offer a long shelf life; similar to glass, they are inert and therefore provide good product protection. Cans are strong, space-efficient, and recyclable.

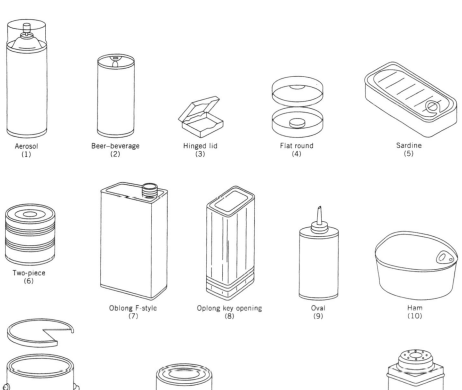

Aerosol
(1)

Beer–beverage
(2)

Hinged lid
(3)

Flat round
(4)

Sardine
(5)

Two-piece
(6)

Oblong F-style
(7)

Oblong key opening
(8)

Oval
(9)

Ham
(10)

Multiple friction
(11)

Three-piece sanitary
(12)

Spice
(13)

Square-breasted
(14)

Can Illustrations

The Wiley Encyclopedia of Packaging Technology. Aaron Brody and Kenneth S. Marsh. 1997. John Wiley & Sons, Inc. Used by permission of John Wiley & Sons, Inc.

Cans are produced in either two-piece or three-piece designs.

Metal Containers

Metal "tins" can be manufactured in a variety of shapes and sizes.

Tubes

Metal tubes are typically made out of aluminum and are frequently used for pharmaceutical and health and beauty products such as creams, gels, ointments, personal lubricants, and other semisolids as well as for adhesives, sealants, caulks, paints, and other home-improvement, household, and industrial products. With special laminates that prevent product interaction, tubes provide effective product protection and are lightweight.

Flexible Packaging

Flexible packaging covers a wide range of structures and materials or combinations of materials, typically paper and plastic that is not rigid. Common flexible forms are bags, pouches, sleeves, and film wraps. Flexible packaging structures are generally filled with product (bread) or wrapped around a structure (soap).

Flexible bags and pouches are typically made from plastic film laminates. Each of the multiple layers of the laminate serves a specific function. The outside layer is ideal for printing and can be made from plastic, metalized film or foil, or paper. Plastic films can be reverse-printed through a process in which the graphics are flipped and printed on the backside or inside (subsurface or buried) to prevent the graphics from deteriorating in the retail environment. The inner layers of a film laminate usually provide barrier protection for the product. Depending on the flexible material and the product composition, multilayer films can maintain a product's shelf life. Although some flexible materials may not be recyclable, they use less packaging material, flatten easily, and take up less room in the waste stream. With new materials, manufacturing, and filling abilities, the flexible film category has grown immensely.

Friskies Cat Snacks Flexible Pouches
The opportunity to produce different contour shapes and use high-quality gravure printing makes flexible packaging stand out on the shelf.

Resealable Pouch
Resealable closures such as zippers maintain product freshness and are widely used in a range of product categories.

**Fuze Beverage Full
Shrink Labels**
Shrink film allows for
complete coverage
of bold high-quality
graphics.

Labels

Usually made of paper, paper laminates, or plastic film with or without an adhesive
backing ("pressure sensitive"), labels can be full-wrap or spot and die-cut in many
different shapes to complement the contour of a structure.

One form of flexible packaging is shrink film used for labeling. This material, when
applied with heat, stretches around the contour of the form it envelops. Plastic
containers, glass bottles, cans, and other rigid structures can be wrapped by this
flexible packaging. The ability for shrink film to be preprinted with all of the packaging
design graphics allows for complete coverage around complex curves and surfaces
that otherwise could not be printed.

Closures

Closures serve as packaging structures used to seal bottles, jars, tubes, and cartons. Some common plastic closures are threaded screw caps and lids, hinged caps, push-pull closures (common on water bottles and squeezable food containers), spray nozzles, and pumps. Metal closures include lug caps, threaded screw caps and lids, overcaps, punched shaker tops, and pull tops. Closures provide resealability, reusability, and recyclability and can provide leak resistance, child-proof protection, and reveal tamper evidence. Some closures are manufactured with foil induction seals to provide barrier protection for a longer shelf life.

Custom-designed closures made in plastic and metal are frequently patented for use by a particular brand or product. Serving to make packaging structures distinctive, closures not only offer new functionality in dispensing a product but provide opportunities for decorative impact on shelf. Closures should be coordinated with packaging graphics and can be made of both plastic and metal.

Stock Packaging

Stock packaging is the term used for structures and materials produced for nonexclusive use that are readily available to the marketer. Glass, plastic, and metal are among the materials used to make "stock" packaging structures or closures. Stock packaging structures are not proprietary for one particular brand or company, meaning that they are available to everyone. With the constant design and manufacturing of new structures and closures, the options for stock packaging have grown immensely.

Paperboard manufacturers offer stock folding cartons, corrugated boxes, set-up boxes, and gift boxes. These structures are available in decorative papers and finishes and a wide array of standard sizes and can be purchased individually or in bulk. Bags, canisters, and cylindrical containers of all shapes, sizes, and configurations in paper and plastic are available as stock packaging structures as well.

For many consumer product companies, stock packaging provides a practical solution as a quick way to get a packaging design to market. An analysis of the product, structure, finish opportunities (embossing, stamping, laminating), and printing limitations for a given design surface is the first step before making the decision to use a stock packaging structure.

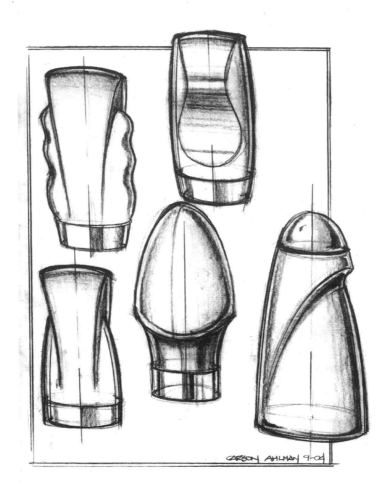

Preliminary Design Sketches of Bottle Structures
Design Firm: Carson Ahlman Design
Industrial Designer: Carson Ahlman

Structural Design

The design and development of a three-dimensional structure for use in packaging design is a discipline unto itself. Typically professionals trained in industrial or structural design, product design, or engineering are the most qualified. These experts are versed in specific materials and may work directly with a manufacturer. Structural designers often specialize in paperboard, plastic, metal, glass, wood, or any range of other materials. Many brand and packaging design firms have structural designers on staff, offering proprietary structural design capabilities to clients.

Structural designers similar to packaging designers need to consider product use, production costs, marketing, and category characteristics to design efficiently and effectively. Being well versed in particular materials and knowing what materials serve specific functions, combined with the ability to visualize three-dimensionally with sketches by hand or via computer, is essential.

Model Making

Some industrial designers have the capacity to create their own three-dimensional prototypes of packaging structures. Others outsource the work to model makers. Model makers and industrial design firms may specialize in specific materials (foam, wood, Lucite, metal) and industry categories (cosmetics, food, beverage, and household products) and many firms are a one-stop-shop that can complete any structural design problem.

Rapid Prototyping

Rapid prototyping (RP) is an automated production tool that creates a three-dimensional prototype through a process by which computer-aided design (CAD) renderings are scanned by a "three-dimensional printer." This time-saving process allows for greater flexibility in the design and exploration of three-dimensional models by allowing for more than one model to be examined before approving the final one.

New Material Technologies

Consumers react to packaging design with their senses of sight and touch. However, new technologies in materials manufacturing are providing more experiential packaging design opportunities to ellicit greater consumer response and physically engage them at the shelf. There are packaging designs that can have smells and also tastes.

ColorWorks Soft Touch® Bottles
Client: ColorWorks New York/Clariant Masterbatches Division

Consumer demand for packaging with a tactile effect was met with "Soft Touch" technology, which was achieved by specifying a polypropylene copolymer for the bottle's thin outside layer using a multilayer blow-molding application.

Since smells are meaningful and visceral, they can invoke memories, experiences, and pleasures; trigger emotion and hunger; and create true impulses. It is not surprising that smell is being incorporated into packaging materials as part of the consumer experience.

New scented inks are making their way onto packages with scratch-and-sniff technology. In this process the ink is encapsulated in a polymer and released upon friction. In addition, new scent delivery systems are being introduced to integrate the scent directly into the printing process by applying it as a clear varnish on top of packaging graphics.

Keeping a keen eye on trends in new manufacturing, materials, and production technology can bring a competitive advantage to creating successful packaging design solutions.

Crest Scratch-and-Sniff Cartons
Through Scratch-and-Sniff technology, consumers can experience new flavors at the shelf for Crest's Whitening Expressions product line.

ScentSational Technologies is the world leader in developing, patenting, and licensing Olfaction Packaging technology. ScentSational utilizes its patented and proprietary Encapsulated Aroma Release® technology to incorporate specially engineered FDA-approved food-grade GRAS (Generally Recognized As Safe) flavors directly into food and beverage packaging components, and fragrances into consumer product packaging. As a result, the packaging essentially becomes aromatized. This technology dramatically enhances the overall consumer experience and creates for a more memorable brand experience. The technology can also serve to resolve myriad problems inherent in plastic packaging, including masking the odors of plastic packaging and mitigating flavor scalping from plastic, therefore extending shelf life.

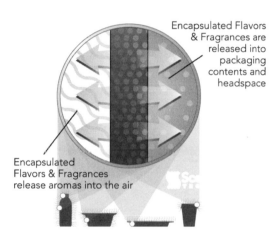

Encapsulated Flavors & Fragrances are released into packaging contents and headspace

Encapsulated Flavors & Fragrances release aromas into the air

CompelAroma®
Company:
ScentSenational
Technologies

The center dark section shows how flavors or fragrances are infused throughout the entire monolayer structure; the technology can be used in multilayer.

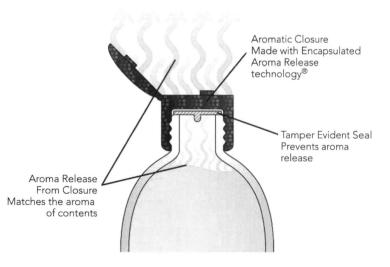

Aromatic Closure Made with Encapsulated Aroma Release technology®

Tamper Evident Seal Prevents aroma release

Aroma Release From Closure Matches the aroma of contents

CompelAroma TE®
Company:
ScentSenational
Technologies

Consumers can experience the aroma of a product, captured and maintained in the closure or tamper seal, without breaking the seal and opening the cap on a bottle.

Key Points about Structures and Materials

✓ Consider the materials and their advantages and disadvantages at the onset of every packaging design assignment.

✓ Understand the size, shape, and structural material of the packaging.

✓ Take into account material performance under retail conditions.

9 PLANNING FOR PRODUCTION

Design Considerations for Materials and Production

The quote by motivational trainer Franklin Covey "begin with the end in mind" is a great philosophy for packaging design. In order to develop responsible packaging designs, production requirements must be carefully considered. The success of a packaging design rests not solely in a marketable concept but also in its ability to be produced and its adaptability to serving a company's broad packaging design needs.

The packaging designer must be fully informed of the:

- size, shape, and structural material of the packaging;
- print specifications for the specific materials;
- material performance under retail conditions;
- software considerations for the computerization of printing and automation of the packaging process;
- global packaging design requirements of the brand, including packaging structural changes, language adaptations, and design modifications.

Production issues should be reviewed and concerns should be addressed with the client and production team before the design process begins. The flow of work between all parties involved in the design process can run smoothly if the significant production issues are addressed up front.

The key production goals are to:

- maintain design integrity and production quality;
- stay on schedule;
- control production costs;
- avoid any unnecessary revisions;
- utilize appropriate technology;
- provide a design solution that is extendable and adaptable.

Starting with the packaging structure—whether it's a paperboard carton, a plastic bottle, a glass jar, or a flexible film pouch—the designer should be familiar with how the packaging design will be printed, how the end product will be filled, and any technical production requirements. It is appropriate to ask detailed questions early in the process. Being fully informed of the production methods for the different types of structures and packaging materials used for the product is essential. Materials play a leading role in the consumer perception of the product in terms of quality, value (price-point), and category appropriateness.

Understanding Technology

In most cases packaging designs are developed in a collaborative, technologically advanced work environment. Computer software is used throughout the entire design process, from the creation of initial design concepts to comp development, all the way through to pre-press production. Adobe Illustrator, Adobe Photoshop, and Adobe InDesign are the primary programs used in packaging design.

Most companies have a system for how the packaging design job flows through the appropriate channels. A work-flow system saves time and money by ensuring that the design, development, and implementation of a packaging design is efficient, managed by the appropriate parties, approved by the client, and ultimately passed on to final production.

File Management

In the packaging design process there can be anywhere from a handful to countless different design concepts developed. Initial concepts may begin as hand-rendered sketches and evolve into digital computer documents. Whether created by a single designer or a team, at some point the files are shared and passed from one work group to another. The correct creation of files and their management throughout the design process can alleviate problems in the work-flow process, and more important, in final production.

File sharing demands the efficiency of work flow: files must be complete with the components needed to launch them into their respective software programs, opening with all imagery, graphic elements, and fonts loaded and properly placed. This allows for designers, departments, and clients to review the development of the creative work.

USE THE LAYER TOOL

Using the layer tool in Adobe Illustrator and Adobe Photoshop is essential and provides the designer with the ability to separate imagery and elements within a document. The use of layers can prevent elements from being misplaced or incorrectly sized in production files, and can make modifications and alterations easier by enabling access to specific elements. The layer tool helps to eliminate the risk of editing the wrong elements.

Art Files: Image vs. Vector

Packaging designs commonly use illustrative and photographic images and graphic elements that need to be captured from their original paper format and saved on a computer file. Understanding the quality of the image resolution—the number of pixels per inch (ppi) on a computer screen or the number of dots per inch (dpi) for printed materials and how many (high, medium, low) are needed for a specific job—is an important initial step in the scanning process. For example, if the image is to be used initially for a rough concept presentation, a lower resolution may be acceptable. The standard for Web-based computer images and "for position only" in a computer file is 72 ppi. If the image may possibly be used for final reproduction art, a higher resolution (300 dpi is standard for printed material) may be required. Although images can be, and often are, manipulated in various software programs (to adjust for color, brightness, contrast, and design elements), ultimately some image files are resolution dependent and need to be created at a high resolution for reproduction.

Files are saved in a number of formats. The general format options for image files (as opposed to text files) are as follows:

TIFF (Tagged Image File Format): A bitmap format used for the exchange of images between applications; can be placed in almost all graphic and layout programs and is commonly used for the storage of an image.

EPS (Encapsulated PostScript): Can represent both vector and bitmap elements, and is supported by many graphic and layout programs.

JPEG (Joint Photographic Experts Group): Used for displaying continuous tone images such as photographs and vector art and is a universal format for Web-based images.

PDF (Portable Document Format): Represents both vector and bitmap elements and is the primary format for Adobe Illustrator® and Adobe Acrobat® (most computers on both Mac and PC operating systems come loaded with Adobe Acrobat® Reader, allowing everyone to read a PDF file). The PDF format is used to send files electronically to colleagues and clients, to pre-press services, or to a printer.

Since file formats vary in terms of end purpose, resolution, color quality, and other technical capabilities, an understanding of the end purpose of the image and file are important considerations for production.

Typography, shapes, and other graphic elements are generally converted to outline or vector art. Vector art, made up of lines, straight and curved, and points, define shapes that can be filled with color. Type brought in as a specific font can be converted to vector art ("Create Outlines," under the Type menu in Adobe Illustrator) and maintains the design characteristics of the typestyle but eliminates the need to load font files with the mechanical for final production. The lines, when converted to vector art, can be "stroked" to have an outline of varying thickness (weight) and color. Vector art is resolution independent, which means it can be scaled to any size and printed without losing its sharpness and detail.

File management includes keeping all of the original art of placed files (Adobe Photoshop® EPS or TIFF files) in an organized folder that is included with all of the mechanical files and may ultimately be sent to a printer. If the typography is not converted to outline or vector format, the original fonts used in the design should be included in the file sent to the printer.

File Naming

Naming files is another aspect of file management. This is where organizing principles apply. The files must include the standard file extension. This is the scheme that is tagged onto the end of the file name that makes files compatible with the operating system and software (i.e., .doc, .ai, .pdf). There should be an appropriate file name that is extendable to various packaging design concepts and editions, and that properly catalogs the documents by revisions and modifications. Since many different people come into contact with these files, the naming system must be one that easily identifies specific documents and files. A disk that is unorganized and has misnamed files requires spending countless hours opening and closing files in an attempt to locate the right one. Files must be named in such a way that all parties can readily gain access.

The Packaging Die

Once the packaging structure and materials are determined, a designer usually receives a digital file of the packaging die from the client or the packaging material supplier. The *die* is the blueprint of the structure or design layout and provides the exact dimensions and production specifications. Bleed requirements and gluing specifications are included in a two-dimensional drawing to which the designer can apply brand information and graphics using computer graphic software. Solid lines represent cut lines and depict the package contours or outside edge; dotted lines represent score lines (of folding cartons, set-up boxes, etc.) made by depressing a metal rule into the outside surface of paperboard or other material to create a crease. The packaging material is then folded on the crease of the score.

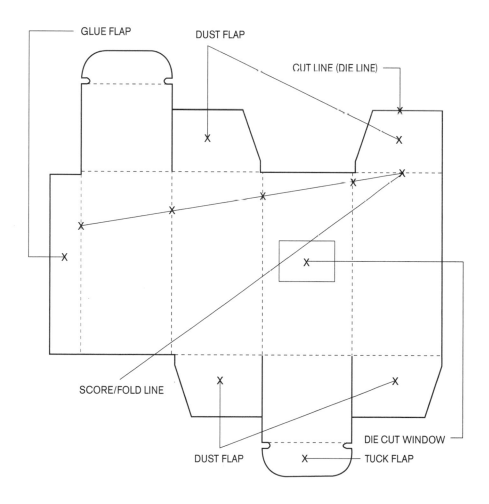

GLUE FLAP

DUST FLAP

CUT LINE (DIE LINE)

SCORE/FOLD LINE

DUST FLAP

TUCK FLAP

DIE CUT WINDOW

**NOTE TO PRINTER: PLEASE USE PROCESS BLUE IN PLACE
AND REFER TO PREVIOUS SEPARATION AN**

CHIP ART PRINTS MYK

15"
CUTOFF
Compensation 97.40%
Photopolymer (.067)

HERR'S RED MATCH

BANNER PRINTS MYK

UPC - FPO

9" FACE

18.75" WEB

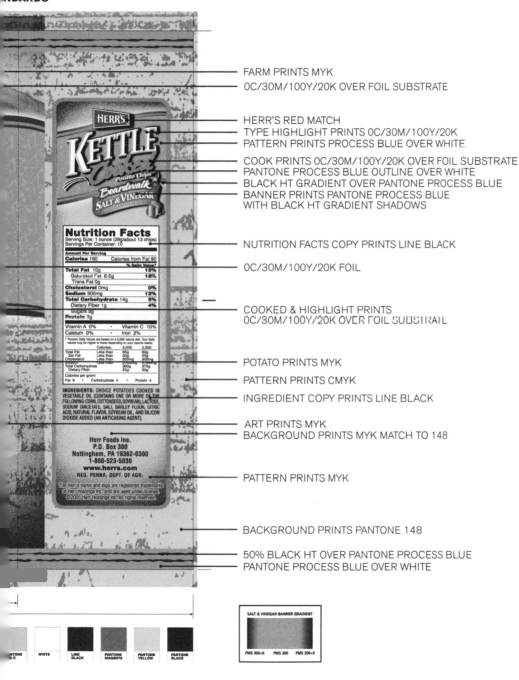

FARM PRINTS MYK
0C/30M/100Y/20K OVER FOIL SUBSTRATE

HERR'S RED MATCH
TYPE HIGHLIGHT PRINTS 0C/30M/100Y/20K
PATTERN PRINTS PROCESS BLUE OVER WHITE

COOK PRINTS 0C/30M/100Y/20K OVER FOIL SUBSTRATE
PANTONE PROCESS BLUE OUTLINE OVER WHITE
BLACK HT GRADIENT OVER PANTONE PROCESS BLUE
BANNER PRINTS PANTONE PROCESS BLUE
WITH BLACK HT GRADIENT SHADOWS

NUTRITION FACTS COPY PRINTS LINE BLACK

0C/30M/100Y/20K FOIL

COOKED & HIGHLIGHT PRINTS
0C/30M/100Y/20K OVER FOIL SUBSTRATE

POTATO PRINTS MYK

PATTERN PRINTS CMYK

INGREDIENT COPY PRINTS LINE BLACK

ART PRINTS MYK
BACKGROUND PRINTS MYK MATCH TO 148

PATTERN PRINTS MYK

BACKGROUND PRINTS PANTONE 148

50% BLACK HT OVER PANTONE PROCESS BLUE
PANTONE PROCESS BLUE OVER WHITE

**Herr's Kettle Chips
Digital Mechanical
of Flexible Snack
Bag**
Client:
Herr Foods
Design Firm:
IQ Design Group
Designer:
Will Rodriguez

The layer sets
and exact file
specifications are
determined by the
specific printing and
finishing processes
for the packaging
design.

The Packaging Mechanical

The digital packaging mechanical is the file or artwork employed by the printer to produce the final packaging design. Once the packaging design die is downloaded in a digital format, the digital mechanical file is ready to be assembled. The mechanical file is assembled with the packaging die being the first layer in a document. All graphic elements, images, and typography are placed on additional layers. The organization of the layers within the mechanical file is dependent on what reproduction processes will be used to create the final packaging design.

File Delivery and Pre-Flight

Pre-flight is the term used for the final inspection made to a file to verify that it is ready for printing. Pre-flight software supports the process of verifying and collecting fonts, images, and other elements that need to be included in the file.

Pre-flight checklist is included the mechanical file with the following:

- correct naming and file extension;
- packaging die with graphic layers;
- appropriate crop marks and bleeds allowances;
- graphic elements formatted properly (as per pre-press service provider/printer);
- deletion of extraneous elements, fonts, and colors from file;
- fonts (only the actual styles used within the family; i.e., bold, italic, regular, and not those specified through software features);
- correct placement of art files (Photoshop EPS or TIFF files);
- images cropped to appropriate sizes for placement;
- print specifications with accurate instructions, including any notes relevant to color specs, special processes for finishing, software versions;
- check on the computer platform and other requirements of the pre-press service provider/printer;
- backup folder of all of the files included in the mechanical.

Digital Work-Flow

With the use of digital technology throughout the production process, the ability to create a networked and automated process is made easier. Work-flow automation allows all aspects of production from pre-press to press to post-press (cutting, scoring) to move through different phases seamlessly.

There are many different systems used to serve digital work-flow management—there is no one "standardized" process or technology. The basic concept is that the printer produces a printing plate directly from the files (CPT—computer-to-plate). This process relies on the highly specialized printing technology called Direct Imaging (DI) and can create a faster (data needs to be input only once), higher-quality, and better managed production system.

In the end, with digital work-flow technology or any other process, the designer should have a clear understanding of what the printer requires for final file delivery.

Color and Printing

Multicolor printing is typical in most packaging designs, with the four-color process being the standard. The four-color process uses four colors of inks—cyan, magenta, yellow, and black (CMYK)—to make up all other printed colors. This is achieved by the creation of dot patterns in different sizes layered at different angles. The size of the dots determines the appearance of the printed colors.

A match color is a specified color of ink. Match colors are determined by established color systems such as the PANTONE MATCHING SYSTEM® (PMS). The application of color and the ability to color match within digital files is achieved through graphic software packages that support the use of PMS.

Match, "spot," or "line" colors provide consistent and accurate color in multiple print runs with different vendors. They can be used alone in one-, two-, and three-color printing jobs or in conjunction with four-color process printing. Often brand logos or specific elements of a brand identity are designed using specific colors. In these design scenarios, where a color has been determined and the accurate color reproduction is critical across all applications, match colors are specified. Since color can vary from print run to print run and printer to printer, color standards must be established to define the acceptable tolerances in color shift on the initial print run. Creating standards will prevent a significant variance in color caused by press quality, press conditions, size of print runs, and differences in materials.

Color requirements are determined by the number of printed colors specified for the job, the printing process, the type of press used, and by costs, budgets, and financial considerations. The use of the standard four colors in the four-color process means that all colors within a digital mechanical file must be converted to CMYK equivalents. Computer software provides the capacity to change colors to CMYK equivalents, but they do not necessarily convert to exact matches. Print tests (color matching between computer screen and print output source; for example, desktop printers) should always be done to check for color accuracy. If spot or match colors are used, they can remain specified as PMS colors within the mechanical file as long as printing limitations and the number of available colors are checked.

Color Management

Color management in packaging design is an area that has become complicated because of computer technology and differing proofing, pre-press, and printing processes. When a file is sent to a client and viewed on a computer screen, the color is viewed differently from screen to screen. When a design is printed, the color varies from printer to printer (and from color on-screen to on-surface) and surface to surface. Everyone in the design approval process must be able to see and approve the same colors. Pre-press color proofs are prepared by the pre-press vendor and, depending on the proofing technology, can be printed on the substrate used for the finished package. These color proofs are a crucial tool in viewing what each color translates to on a given substrate and as it would appear on final packaging design. Color proofing should take place throughout the design process, from client review of packaging design concepts through final mechanical files. The review of final color proofs provides the means of checking layouts, color breaks, registration, typography (copy check for typos, etc.), and final separation quality (especially on photographic or illustrative images) before the job moves into print production.

Printing Processes

The printing processes used for most packaging design materials (paper and paperboard, plastics, flexible films, film and paper laminates, and metal) include:

- Offset Lithography (offset)
- Flexography (flexo)
- Gravure
- Letterpress

Offset Lithography: Web or Sheetfed

Offset lithography is the dominant printing process in packaging design. This process is "planographic," meaning the printing plates carry both the image and non-image areas on the same level (in gravure printing images are recessed, and in letterpress printing image areas are raised). Offset lithography is based on the principle of oil repelling water off a surface. A photochemical process is used to transfer the image onto a plate that accepts oil-based inks and repels water. The inked image is "offset" to a rubber blanket that transfers the image onto the printing surface: the printing surface does not directly contact the plate. The resilience of the rubber blanket makes it possible to print on a wide variety of surfaces.

Traditionally offset presses were sheetfed (single sheets of paper or substrate); but now presses can be web run on continuous rolls of paper, and some presses can print both sides simultaneously. High-speed web presses are typically used for high-volume printing of newspapers, books, and direct mail. With offset lithography the graphic quality is excellent for both long- and short-run jobs.

With technological advances in pre-press and press procedures, lithographic plates can be produced directly from computer design software for "direct-to-plate" (DTP) printing, eliminating films and processing. Direct-to-plate printing saves time and money, but most important it is an environmentally sensitive choice as it reduces the use of hazardous chemicals used for plate making.

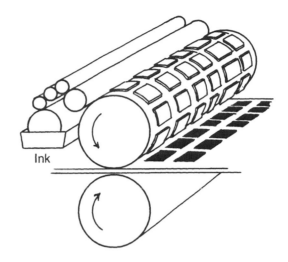

Ink

Flexography

Flexography or "flexo" is a printing process used on a wide variety of packaging materials. Corrugated containers, folding cartons, paper and plastic bags, milk cartons, plastic containers, labels, tags, flexible films, and foils are often printed with this method. The use of flexible rubber or plastic printing plates, similar to letterpress, produces a raised image area that carries the ink. Rotated on a cylinder, the plates transfer the image to the packaging substrate. Flexo was once considered a lower-quality process; however, improved technology now rivals that of offset and gravure for some applications. With the wide use of water-based inks, this process has gained merit for its environmentally safe quality.

According to the William C. Dowdell, former president of the Flexographic Technical Association (FTA), "Flexo has become the dominant print method in the packaging industry." One of the advantages of flexography in packaging is its adaptability for short print runs. "Consumer product companies are so focused on the market that packaging has been elevated to a key point in advertising strategy, particularly as a means to address demographic segments. Consumer product companies are asking for smaller orders, which favors flexo's ability to produce shorter runs. In the past, a company would lock into one image campaign and use that throughout the company. Now the idea is that a consumer product company will change the image they use depending on the demographics of the area they are targeting."

Dry offset or offset flexography is widely used for printing on metal cans and preformed plastic cups, tubs, and tubes. Dry offset flexography can be used to print large volumes of multicolor full-process art at high speeds. This process differs from regular offset because it is waterless and uses special inks. The absence of water requires advanced cooling equipment and special printing plates.

Lithography Schematic
The Packaging Designer's Book of Patterns. George L. Wybenga and László Roth. 2003. John Wiley & Sons, Inc. Used by permission of John Wiley & Sons, Inc.

The inked image is "offset" to a rubber blanket that transfers the image onto the printing surface: the printing surface does not directly contact the plate.

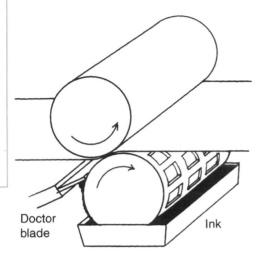

Gravure Schematic
The Packaging Designer's Book of Patterns.
George L. Wybenga and Lászlo Roth. 2003. John Wiley & Sons, Inc. Used by permission of John Wiley & Sons, Inc.

The etched areas are engraved into cylinders that carry ink, producing the image on the paper's surface.

Gravure/Rotogravure

The gravure printing process is the opposite of letterpress in that etched areas are engraved into cylinders that carry ink, producing the image on the paper's surface. Thousands of tiny recessed cells of varying sizes and depths determine how much ink is transferred onto the paper as it is passes between a gravure cylinder and an impression cylinder. Gravure printing tends to be the most expensive printing process due to set-up or "make-ready" time and the cost of plate making. Rotogravure is the same process using paper on large rolls rather than individual sheets. The gravure process produces consistent high-quality printing that serves well for multicolor process designs that are typically used on large runs with high production speeds. High-end packaging designs, art books, and magazines all achieve high-quality graphics using this process.

Gravure printing produces high-quality graphics on shrink film and can achieve the etched or frosted look of glass. These and other effects on printed shrink film labels can save time and be a cost-saving alternative to the expensive processes of glass manufacturing.

Letterpress

Letterpress, the oldest form of printing, is a relief process in which the image is raised on a metal plate that carries the ink and transfers it directly to the substrate. It is often used for short runs of stationery, greeting cards, invitations, special-edition books, and other specialty designs or in combination with other processes, such as embossing. Photoengraving (acid etching) was the way the image was formed onto the metal plate in the past but today photo-polymer plates made of metal and hard plastic are used. Letterpress printing produces clean, sharp type and high-quality imagery, although halftones are somewhat inferior to offset because of coarser line screens.

"Digital printing is an imaging process where all graphic content is in digital form from creation to output." (Digital Printing Council, May 2005) Digital printing used to mean straight from the desktop on your laser printer, but has moved beyond that as technology continues to advance. Loosely defined, the term *digital printing* refers to the processes used to print a final piece. Digital printing is evolving and traditional processes are declining, reducing time and cost and providing a safer alternative for the environment.

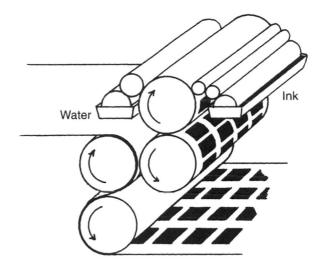

Water

Ink

Letterpress Schematic
The Packaging Designer's Book of Patterns.
George L. Wybenga and László Roth. 2003. John Wiley & Sons, Inc.
Used by permission of John Wiley & Sons, Inc.

The image is raised on a metal plate that carries the ink and transfers it directly to the substrate.

Each printing process has its own set of performance considerations and limitations. The material to be printed with quality, quantity (how big the print run is), color requirements (how many colors/type of press), make-ready (pre-press preparation) time, cost, and location being some of the factors that determine which process is used.

Special Processes and Techniques

Screen Printing

Screen printing, based on stenciling, is most suitable for one- and two-color printing. Materials that can be screened include paper and paperboard, plastic, wood, metal, glass, fabric, and leather. A screen with a fine mesh material, originally silk, stretched across a wooden or metal frame, is used with an impermeable stencil. In commercial screen printing, the stencil is created and applied to the screen using a photosensitized emulsion coating. Paper stencils can be used, or the image can be drawn directly on the screen with varnish. The screen is placed on the material to be printed, and ink is drawn across the stencil, thereby transferring the design. The ink passes only through the image area of the stencil. There is a screen that corresponds to each color. Successive layers of colors are added for more complex images. Precise registration, or exact positioning, of each subsequent layer on the substrate is critical.

Embossing

Embossing is the creation of a relief, or raised image, on the surface of paperboard or other packaging materials by running it through a pair of dies in the shape of the image. Pressure and heat reshapes the surface of the paper to create the image. Dies can be made of metal, paperboard, and even felt (for fabric embossing), depending on the material to be embossed. Different kinds of embossing include single, multilevel, and beveled styles and can be combined with ink, images, or foil for special effects. The same process achieves debossing, but the surface is depressed from the front side. Embossing on glass and plastic is an integral part of the molding process.

Hot (Foil) Stamping

Hot stamping is a method of decorating by transferring an image in a thin layer of film or foil onto paperboard or plastic by means of heat and pressure. The image is released from a carrier film to the paperboard or plastic substrate by the heated die pressed against it, creating a laminate. Type, logos, and other graphic images are typically hot stamped.

Bawls Guarana Bottle
Client:
Hobarama Corp.
Design Firm:
Flowdesign
Designer:
Dan Matauch

This highly caffeinated beverage bottle, with its knobby surface texture, gives the glass a unique tactile feel.

Varnishes and Coatings

Varnishes and coatings are used to create visual effects using glossy, dull, and matte finishes. Varnishes can seal ink and protect printed substrate surfaces from scuffing and rubbing off. Varnishes are petroleum-based and are applied as a standard color station on press. Spot varnishing is a technique applied to specific areas on photographs or other graphic images that uses a glossy varnish to contrast a dull printed surface. This result of a spot varnish can make the glossy image pop, and when used on a one-color design can create a unique effect. Varnishes provide a flexible coating without the risk of ink bleeding underneath and can be used on any weight substrate.

Aqueous coatings are another means of ink rub-off protection for packaging designs. Available in matte, dull, satin, and gloss finishes, these water-based layers can be used on heavyweight papers and substrates. Ultraviolet coatings offer the same finishes as aqueous coatings. They are exposed and dried by UV radiation almost instantaneously, speeding up press time and providing the best (but the most expensive) rub-off protection.

Rex Corporation Promotional Cartons
Firm:
Rex Corporation
Designers:
Joanna Tak,
Rina Minosky

These promotional cartons showcase the possibility of litho-printed SBS, foil, and rainbow holographic paperboard. Printing consisted of a gloss UV flood coat with a matte varnish pattern coat; the application of matte varnish on top of the UV coating reticulates to leave a dull finish, adding depth and interest.

In-Mold Labeling (IML) for Plastics

Pressure-sensitive and glue-application labels, shrink-sleeve labels, heat-transfer foils and decals are all conventional methods of labeling and decorating injection-molded plastic containers as well as glass bottles. Traditionally this process happens after the containers have been manufactured (post-mold).

IML is a predecoration process used in blow-molded and injection-molded bottles and containers in which the label is placed in the open mold and held there while plastic resin is extruded or injected into the mold. Labels are held in place by vacuum ports or electrostatic charges. The label becomes an integral part of the structure—it's on the surface but in the wall of the plastic container. In blow molding, label materials typically are printed films made of the same material as the container (polyester, varieties of polyethylene and polypropylene), protected on the front surface with a UV (ultraviolet) or EB (electronic beam) curable coating with a heat-seal adhesive layer on the back for blow molding. The heat-sealed layer fuses with the container during the molding process. Polypropylene is used for both container and label in injection molding. High temperatures used during the molding process fuse the label without the need for a heat-seal coating on the back of the film.

Technological advances have provided for a one-step process that produces a fully labeled component directly into the packaging structure. Images such as photographs and illustrations can become embedded labels rather than applied to the outer surface of the packaging structure. Through this process the label takes on a structural as well as a decorative value, the packaging can be as much as 15 percent lighter, and the sidewall of the packaging can be strengthened.

Applied Ceramic Labeling (ACL) for Glass

ACL is another "no-label" look and is a process where ceramic powders mixed with thermoplastic chemicals (which become ink when heated) are applied to glass containers by screen printing. This ceramic ink contains glass (and may contain heavy metals like lead, cadmium, and chromium) and is fired onto bottles as they pass through a conveyer oven under intense heat.

Newer ultraviolet inks and spray enamels are eliminating the use of high heat and have other benefits—no heavy metals in their composition, organic pigments that achieve brighter colors, curing with UV light at a much lower temperature—all of which make them better for the environment. These inks can be applied to produce patterns and other graphic elements or can be used to coat the entire bottle, giving it a frosted effect in place of etching. This type of application is now called "cold color decorating."

Boylan Soda Bottles
These nostalgic soda bottles are printed ACL, giving them a classic old-time appearance.

ACL graphics can be created with up to three colors and can be applied 360 degrees around the surface. They are raised after fusing with the bottle's surface and have a slight embossed look. They are resistant to scuffing and scraping, and are an alternative to other labeling devices for cosmetic containers because they resist alcohol and oils and to glass beverage bottles because of their permanency and water-resistance.

Acid Etching for Glass

Acid etching is a process of "frosting" glass. Etching dissolves the surface of the glass with the application of hydrofluoric acid to the surface. Etching creates a satin matte finish similar to that of sandblasting. Graphic patterns and other elements can be produced by coating the glass with wax and scratching, or scribing, the image through the wax like a stencil. The areas that have been scratched away will be etched. The inherent danger of using the highly corrosive acid has forced the development of new procedures that reduce hazardous working conditions and address environmental concerns.

Production Follow-Through

Packaging design production is dependent on a logical process and an understanding of the different types of printing technology. Packaging designs that cannot be translated into printable mechanicals or do not provide for flexibility across product-line extensions, materials, structures, or substrates are useless. Every design must fit within the production system and requirements.

Production standards provide the framework for the how the packaging design digital files will flow through the system. As packaging designs reach their final phase of design and move to production, the setting of printing standards at the initial press run is an important step. Production managers that handle printing and purchasing from consumer products companies or that work for the printer are sources for guidance in how to achieve the optimal printed packaging design. Revisions and adjustments to a packaging design happen throughout the process. Critical changes that occur on press can alter a packaging design from a cost and/or design perspective. Setting guidelines and standards and creating a clear channel of communication are integral to the end result.

Key Points about Production

✓ Consider production issues at the onset of a design assignment.

✓ Utilize appropriate print specifications for the specific materials.

✓ Maintain design integrity and production quality.

✓ Stay on schedule.

✓ Control production costs.

✓ Avoid any unnecessary revisions.

✓ Employ appropriate technology.

✓ Provide a design solution that is extendable and adaptable.

10 THE DESIGN PROCESS

The Marketing Brief

An understanding of the design process is essential for anyone involved in the business of packaging design. The methodology that defines how an idea for a product results in a packaging design that ultimately lands in the hands of a consumer is complex. The process begins with need for the physical containment of the product and clearly defined marketing objectives for selling the product.

The strategic marketing objectives are best defined in what is termed the *marketing brief*. This document is the first stage in understanding the marketing strategy and retail objectives for a product or brand. It is a straightforward and comprehensive report that summarizes all of the vital information needed for the creative team to understand the nature and scope of the work. The document should be directional but also open-ended to allow for the exploration of a wide range of design directions. A marketing brief that visually "paints a picture" of the marketer's objectives advances the design conceptualization process.

The marketing brief provides:
- background information about the company and the brand;
- the nature and scope of the project (product personality);
- market research (trends, competition);

- the target market (demographics, consumer insights);
- the timetable;
- budget and cost issues;
- production issues and constraints;
- regulatory issues;
- environmental policies.

Large consumer products companies often provide comprehensive marketing briefs that include the compilation of extensive qualitative and quantitative product research. The quantitative research can include collection and analysis of factual data used for market assessment. Qualitative research can provide information collected from interviews with individual consumers or from small (focus) groups. This research takes into account the quality or emotional aspects (including consumer values, attitudes, and reactions) of the product.

A brief that provides an array of consumer insights relevant to the project can be an essential component of the design process. This information provides an understanding of consumer lifestyles, shopping patterns, habits, aesthetic style, and attitudes, and is another meaningful way to help the design team begin to visualize the market.

When a client does not provide the creative team with a marketing brief, or the brief is not exceptionally detailed, the onus is on the designer to ask the questions necessary to understand the key marketing issues for a given project. The better informed the creative team is at the beginning of the assignment, the greater the probability that the final outcome will meet and exceed the client's expectations.

Request for Proposals (RFP)

The marketing brief is often submitted to a number of design firms and a Request For Proposals (RFP) is the next stage in choosing and working with creative consultants. Design firms respond with capabilities presentations in which they present their work and their approach to solving diverse assignments. At this time both parties discuss the project management process, working methods, billing cycles, and client liaisons. Selected firms are then asked to submit proposals.

The Design Proposal

A design proposal communicates how the project will be executed by defining the methodology and identifying the deliverables at specific points in the process. Approval requirements, costs, fees, and expenses are all included in the design proposal. The reiteration of the marketing objectives for the packaging design assignment can help to ensure that both parties have a common understanding of the project and a defined means of communication between the client, design team, suppliers, and vendors. This means determining how work is to be submitted for approvals and how information is to be shared, whether through email or face-to-face meetings. Confidentiality agreements should also be resolved at this stage since these help to define ownership and representational issues. When the proposal is submitted both parties should discuss any extenuating issues or concerns with the project.

The design proposal outlines:

- Design methodology
    Phase One: Research and Analysis
    Phase Two: Preliminary Design
    Phase Three: Design Development
    Phase Four: Final Design Refinement/Comprehensives
    Phase Five: Pre-Production and Digital Mechanicals
- Project terms
    Meeting/deliverable schedule
    Fees and expenses
    Subcontracted services (suppliers, illustration, photography, production, printing)
    Production schedule

The extensiveness of the design proposal depends on the project objectives, the client and the client's budget, and the designer or design firm.

Determining Fees

Packaging design fees differ from firm to firm and are often dictated by the consumer product category and comparable projects. There are myriad considerations for determining project fees: the scope of the assignment, the size of the client, and the size of the design firm are some of the basic issues.

Fees can be defined for each phase or based on an hourly or daily rate, or the entire project can be assigned one fixed fee. Fee terms can include payment schedules, estimated costs and expenses (this covers presentation materials, scanning, comps, art supplies, product samples, courier services, travel and other miscellaneous costs). Expenses covering the creation of original art with photography or illustration and printing or other production costs may be included or can be estimated separately. In addition, issues related to the billing cycle, design ownership, and a cancellation policy should be incorporated into the initial fee terms. There are pros and cons to each fee structure. The creative team and the client should agree on what is mutually suitable for both parties.

Agreement of Terms

The design proposal is reviewed by the client and assessed for its presentation of project scope, its demonstration of a mutually beneficial working relationship, and its fees and terms.

Once the design proposal has been approved (agreement of terms) and signed by the client, it becomes a legal document that protects both parties, keeping them on-track with the project. Any client changes made to the proposal once the project is under way—for example, if additional work is requested or if there are changes in marketing objectives—could warrant supplemental fees since these changes could affect both the project schedule and the deliverables.

Beginning the Assignment

With the delivery of the marketing brief to the designer or design firm and the reciprocal written proposal approved and signed by the client, there is usually a team orientation meeting that involves all stakeholders responsible for the packaging design development. The most important role for the designer or design firm is to provide creative leadership and to keep the strategic objectives and the target market as the focal point throughout the project.

The roles of all the stakeholders are as follows:

- Marketer provides the objectives
- R&D (Research and Development) provides appropriate information on the product's attributes
- Structural engineer provides manufacturing guidelines and final engineering drawings for the physical packaging
- Production develops the final output for printing
- Purchasing procures packaging materials and printing
- Operations directs the manufacturing, filling/packing, and distribution of the product
- Advertising agency provides insight on advertising and promotion

PHASE 1: Research and Analysis

Once all of the initial marketing issues have been defined, resolved, and reviewed, the research and analysis phase of the packaging design process begins.

Since products often evolve into lines of products (line extension), an understanding of the long-term strategic objectives for a product can be an essential component in planning for the future of the brand. This includes how the product fits within the overarching brand hierarchy, taking into account the product as part of a large line of products or the only product within the brand, the global marketing goals, and the long-range life goals for the product.

A redesign may be initiated to change an existing packaging design to reflect:

- modification to the product contents;
- change in the packaging material or structure;
- transformation to remain visually competitive within the category;
- addition of a foreign language for global marketing;
- modification of copy or legal requirements.

Questions that affect the redesign include the following:

- What are the strengths or equities of the existing brand?
- What are the equity elements in the packaging design that need to be maintained?
- Have there been changes in this category?
- Does the brand need a face-lift to remain current?
- Does the brand need repositioning to remain competitive or maintain market share?

Phase One Checklist:

- Category Characteristics
- Category Trends
- Environmental Opportunities
- Existing Brand Equities
- Government and Regulatory Requirements
- Packaging Structure
- Product Cost
- Product Positioning
- Retail Channels
- Shelf Positioning/Competition
- Target Customer
- Technical Considerations

Category Analysis

An extensive survey of the product category is necessary to understand the strengths, weaknesses, and overall effectiveness of the competition. Competitive information can provide clues to what attracts the target consumer and can be a means toward uncovering design approaches that can provide a competitive advantage. Most product categories have a "look" that define them. Color, typographic personality, the use of graphic elements, structure, and materials all contribute to the visual definition of the category and its characteristics. Analyzing what is most successful on the shelf will help to create the personality of a new packaging design. In contrast, designing against what is typical in a category can be one approach to creating something distinctive that has greater impact. Understanding the opportunities for new brands and trends within the category while keeping in mind the target consumer, the perceived value of the product, and its actual cost are important considerations at this stage. Creative ideas will come through the research and information-gathering process.

Product Analysis

Serious consideration also should be given to how the product functions since functionality ultimately affects consumers' purchasing decisions. Primary and secondary functions should be assessed, including reliability, accessibility (how it opens and dispenses), optimal use of materials, use of shelf space, ergonomic benefit of the structure, product and packaging after-use, and environmental impact.

Product analysis should include an understanding of the type of packaging material used. Whenever possible consideration should be given to environmental issues, including opportunities to use sustainable, recyclable, biodegradable, or reusable packaging materials. The physical structure is an integral component in the marketing communication of brand and should be given consideration at the onset of the assignment.

Brand Name

In most cases the brand name is the single most important element of a packaging design because it initiates the relationship between the brand and the target consumer audience. The brand name identifies the brand and the product, supports the promise of the brand, and ideally creates a distinctive and memorable impression that becomes the foundation for building brand equity and value in the minds of consumers. Considerable time should be given to thinking about visually interpreting the brand name and developing a range of intial design solutions.

Name Generation

Name generation maybe a critical first step in developing a new brand or product. The task of coming up with a product name is a serious component to a packaging design assignment. Designers may be invited to participate with the client, a brand name consultancy, or in some cases may have full responsibility for name development. Naming is an involved process where balancing objectivity and strategy with subjectivity and emotion is critical.

Typically, making a list of words that are associated with the product and its perceived personality is the best way to begin. The goal is to use a dictionary and thesaurus and look through magazines and newspapers to search for words that are distinctive and memorable. Combining words and letters can make new words. The names of cars, for example, are often made-up words that conjure up a visual image but have no real meaning, such as Alantra, Jetta, and Sentra. Consumer research, category audits, trademark searches, and other search tools help to cull down the word lists. Using a mixture of creative considerations and market research, the final name should clearly reflect the positioning of the product, be memorable, and be aesthetically pleasing and easy for consumers to say and remember. Research conducted by Wharton marketing professor Barbara E. Kahn and Boston College marketing professor Elizabeth G. Miller discovered that in the area of product names, odd names work best in products that rely on the senses, such as food or fashion, but would probably not work in product categories such as health care. However, naming products is a complex skill and at some point the power of even an odd name can wear off as people get use to it. The key to product naming is that even though it may have no real meaning the name should elicit a positive consumer response.

· SWANK ?
· I AM
randy—
· IDENTITY
· gobbledygook
· STRIVE
phunk
· RANT —

– Stinky boy
– CONCRETE
– shampu
· Shabby ✓
· TRU ✓
· HYDROLIX ✓
· RUCKUS ✓

· Maneframe
(main) ?
· rave
· MEDUSA
· FLUX IN FLUX
· Q
· IMPULSE
   PULSE
· INSANITY
· ICE
· JAM

Name Generation
Miscellaneous words jump-start the development of a brand name for teen hair care.

PHASE 1

Visual References or "Swipes"

Building a "swipe" file is an important component of Phase One. A swipe is a visual reference collected for a specific assignment. A swipe file becomes a valuable resource not only for design inspiration but for situating the visual essence of the product or brand. Swipes can be graphic designs, typographic styles, photographs, illustrations taken from labels, hang tags, advertisements, postcards, invitations, magazine clippings, or wallpaper patterns. This resource is used as a starting point for layout, style, and format and helps advance idea generation, design techniques, and creative approaches. Developing graphic elements, typography, and imagery can all be given a new twist or put into a different context through visual reference sources. A swipe file is a good way to get the creative juices flowing, makes visualizing the personality of the product easier, and makes beginning the design process less daunting.

When looking at typographic references, examine the letterforms within each family of type in variations of style, the individual character contours and nuances, ligatures, layout styles, contrast between weights and cases, and color choices. When exploring illustration, look at various styles from photo-realistic, representative, or abstract styles to the many mediums, from pencil, pastel, watercolor, oils, acrylics, markers, and computer renderings. Consider textures, backgrounds, patterns, and colors and how elements can be used in relation to others in a layout to create a distinctive look. Consider the sizing, cropping, and positioning as well as lighting and perspective. Everything in the environment—from the gargoyle on a building to the imprint of a manhole cover on a street—can be a source of visual inspiration.

Swipes and Inspiration
Designer: Adrienne Muken/FIT (Fashion Institute of Technology)

Visual references can be anything from postcards, graphic elements, typographic treatments to illustrations and photographs.

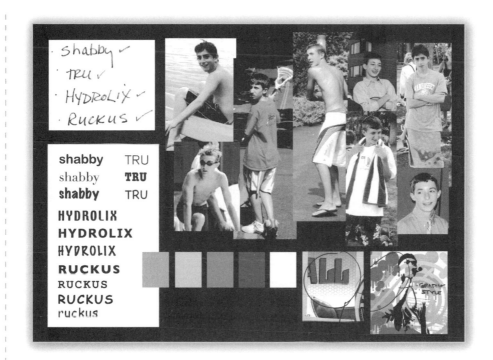

Concept Board
A concept board developed for a personal-care product line targeted toward young teen boys.

Concept Boards

The terms *concept, mood, image, brand essence,* and *user imagery board* refer to the organized collage created from the swipes or visual references that help to communicate the character of the design direction. Created by the creative team, a concept board can convey the style and personality of the target customer, the various colors that fit the vision of the product's personality, the materials that suit the structure, the look of the target consumer or an array of imagery that captures the essence of the brand. A concept board can be created by positioning the swipes in a neat and orderly collage format or on the computer with scanned and positioned images. A concept board is an important tool for the design team to visually formulate a personality for the product; and when presented to the client it can be an integral tool to help the client visualize the marketing and packaging design strategy.

TIME MANAGEMENT

Time management is among the most critical issues throughout the design process. In the beginning of the process the thorough investigation and exploration required to understand the target consumer is often not given enough time. In Phase One research should be conducted in order for the creative team to become immersed in the world of the target consumer. Researching books and magazines, physically going to the marketplace where the consumer shops, watching television programs and movies, listening to the music that the target consumer listens to, researching trends, and visiting the library is all part of becoming entrenched in the product's personality, its competition, and the retail environment in which it is to function. Doing the homework may take time, but is time well spent in the long term since it will enable the designer to better visualize opportunities and solutions.

On the other hand, spending too much time in research that isn't applicable to the packaging design assignment can mean wasted hours and days not focused on the right task. The biggest time waster is getting hung up surfing the Internet pulling up articles and Web sites that don't provide relevant information. Time-management skills are an essential tool.

Keeping a time sheet, daily log, or journal of hours spent on a project is a way to stay on top of how time is managed through the entire creative process. In many firms, time sheets are a requirement and help the budgeting process. Managing the creative process in an efficient manner can mean more dollars earned per hour for the designer and better use of resources for the client.

PHASE 2: Preliminary Design

Beginning a Design Strategy

The preliminary design phase begins with a strategy or plan that provides the map for achieving the visual problem-solving goal. Although in packaging design the overarching marketing strategy is determined by the clients' objectives, there should be more than one design direction or strategy developed in this phase. A clearly articulated packaging design strategy is applied to all aspects of the design concept from the choice of typeface, imagery, and color to that of the structural form. The more design strategies explored, the greater the chances of developing a concept that meets the clients' expectations.

The formulation and development of ideas takes shape from the foundation of research, exploration, and investigation that began in Phase One. Creativity is the key objective of Phase Two, which means discarding any preconceived ideas about how a design should take shape. Every creative idea should be considered in this early stage of the design process. Deliberate, and even provocative questions should be asked, and all ideas should be considered viable since some of the best concepts develop, grow, and change from what was initially perceived as an "okay" idea.

Design is a fluid process. Although a clearly articulated and defined strategy facilitates the process and objective of a successful packaging design, the parameters or design phases are not set in stone. Going back and forth and asking questions throughout the process is part of designing.

Brainstorming and Ideation Sessions

Conceptualizing, brainstorming, and experimenting are among the thinking tools utilized in packaging design to develop concepts. Brainstorming, the random thought process of ideation or the generation of ideas, either individually or in small groups, can be a way to inspire new concepts and ways of thinking. In this process everything that comes to mind with regard to the specific design assignment is written down, from any immediate association with the product, name, structure, category, and target market to subconscious connections made with the product or category. Making lists of adjectives can help in this stage. Do not self-edit or weed out; what one person thinks is unsuitable, another may find a fascinating concept. The brainstorming process should not be rushed. Some of the greatest ideas come when there seems to be nothing left to consider.

Taking notes and keeping a journal will help record ideas and allow for the concepts to be explored. Talk to everyone about the ideas. Use family and friends as sounding boards, and consider their ideas and comments as viable. Explore everything, still keeping in mind the target consumer. Designers should be fully engaged with the world around them. When every visual is filtered through our individual perception of the world we develop our own internal visual thesaurus.

It is not uncommon to be stuck and unable to think creatively. To get out of a design rut, walk, listen to music, exercise, look at visually rich magazines and books, go window shopping, and explore new things. Clear the mind and let ideas filter in for the next inspiration.

Brainstorming can lead to solid design concepts; initial random thoughts evlolve into conceptual directions. As concepts start to develop, think strategically. Ask questions such as the following: What approach does the competition take to market to their audience? What are the points of distinction that this product can convey in its design? How does this idea relate to the marketing objectives?

Concepts and Strategies

Concept and strategy are dependent upon each other. A *concept* is the main idea of a specific design that serves to visually communicate a design strategy. This purposeful design scheme is often developed from brainstorming and is the way to visually execute an idea.

Strategic thinking becomes the rationale for a clearly articulated concept. Concepts that reflect a fresh perspective or a radical approach to the assignment can be a way to stand out in a category. Each packaging design concept should be ingenious, inventive, exemplify creativity, and ultimately grab a consumer's attention. Although appropriateness is critical for the product's packaging design to be effective, to fit into the category, and to elicit the target consumers' attention, the exploration of design concepts should ensue without being too constrained by practicalities.

Each strategic direction could be explored further as one of the initial design concepts. Since each direction can be interpreted and visually communicated in so many ways, there could easily be several packaging design concepts that come from just one of these design strategies.

Words that can help to define strategic directions:

- Authentic
- Celebrity
- Classic
- Conservative
- Contemporary
- Convenient
- Earth-friendly/Green
- Educational
- Experiential
- Family/Friends
- Fantasy
- Futuristic
- Handmade
- Health Conscious

- High-tech
- Gender-specific
- Illustrative
- Luxury
- Minimal
- Old World
- Photographic
- Retro
- Traditional
- Travel
- Trendy
- Typographic
- Unexpected/Surprising
- Urban

TWO DESIGN STRATEGIES

An experiential design strategy could include a sound chip embedded in the packaging design that is activated by opening the structure or by motion. The packaging structure could have a scent infused into the material or a "scratch-and-sniff" area applied to the front. The packaging design could incorporate a 3-D visual illusion such as the use of holographic paper or foil stamping, or could be made of a tactile material or in an ergonomic form that provides a distinct physical experience.

An organic product would probably have an environmentally focused design strategy. This strategy may use eco-friendly, sustainable, and recyclable or reduced use of materials. The design could reflect this strategy graphically through the use of earth tones such as sand, clay, and stone and imagery that communicates this direction. The printing of the packaging design would use digital technology that reduces toxic waste and soy inks that are safer for the environment. The product or its packaging design could have an after-use and be perceived to have added value to the consumer.

PHASE 2

Sketching in Black and White

In general, concepts in Phase Two of the design process should be resolved in black-and-white. There are a number of reasons for this. A concept that has a strong presence in black-and-white will most likely convert well into color; the reverse, however, does not hold true. A color and the success or failure of its application can inhibit the design review process. Inappropriate or ineffective color use could impair the communication of a design concept, forcing it to be rejected even though the overall design may be successful. With the goal of getting as many ideas down on paper quickly in this phase, the application of color is too time-consuming. Remember that in the concept-development stage the more ideas generated, the more likely one or a combination of some will fit the strategy.

Logotype Development

The development of a logotype for the brand identity begins with a wide exploration of typography and visual elements that through their distinctive style suggests the brand's personality. Typestyles communicate different characteristics, and the typographic choices should communicate the brand's personality, be legible, and be unique. Since the logotype for a consumer product is often applied to a wide range of packaging structures and additional printed materials, the design of the brand identity needs to be easily adaptable and legible for different sizes, formats, colors, and print options.

The choices and applications of typography and graphic elements (symbols, icons, and characters—executed in graphic, illustrative or photographic styles) is a significant design challenge. The goal is to create a design that is appropriate, recognizable, and unique to the brand. The brand identity development process can be gratifying when the type choice and design modification clearly resolve the communication objective.

Logo Development
Designer: Theresa Mesce/ FIT (Fashion Institute of Technology)

Quick black and white logo sketches communicate the typographic personality of a brand.

Thumbnail Development

Once some solid concepts have been developed for the brand identity of a product, the layout of the front or primary display panel (PDP) of the packaging design becomes the next consideration, and are sketched in a thumbnail format. Thumbnails are small rough sketches quickly put down onto paper as a means of generating initial ideas, logo concepts, and layouts. Thumbnails are generally carried out using one-color pen or pencil on tracing paper in a bound sketchbook or on a layout pad. Thumbnails should be created in a scaled-down replica of the size and shape of the front or primary display panel. This enables the sketches to accurately reflect the size of the packaging design. Thumbnails are a way of getting a lot of ideas down on paper.

The organization of typography and graphic elements should be done effectively with quick sketches in this phase. Although the rendering of exact typefaces and graphic elements are not important in thumbnails, sketching a rough style that depicts the difference between a serif and san serif typeface and suggesting an image in a layout can help to define the visual communication.

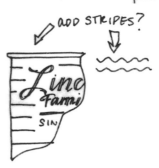

Lindsay Olives Thumbnail Development
Client:
Lindsay Olives
Design Firm:
Addis Design
Creative Director:
Steven Addis
Designer:
Debbie Smith

The layout of typography and graphic elements communicates effectively through these quick thumbnail sketches.

PHASE 2

Initial Layouts

The initial layouts are created based on a review of the most viable thumbnails or rough sketches. In the development of initial layouts, ideas and concepts are explored in more detail. Varying concepts can reflect specific marketing objectives in different ways. Also called preliminary sketches, these designs should be approximate depictions of all of the elements that are required on the final packaging design without being overly analytical or critical of the details. Putting all ideas down on paper and keeping the design development broad but strategic is the best method.

This preliminary design phase should incorporate a wide range of typography, graphic elements, and color with every element supporting the design concept. There are a number of solutions to any given assignment, and each one can have meaningful strategic distinctions. In this phase anywhere from 10 to 15 concepts are realistic, depending on the project, the client, and the budget. Creating one idea with many variations is not the way to achieve a successful range of packaging design solutions. It is critical to refer to the key marketing objectives and, more important, the target consumer as these factors affect the choice of typographic style and color, graphic personality, and marketable concepts.

The following are some examples of the many ways to conceptualize packaging designs:

Clean: The appearance is simple, straightforward, and well organized.

Repeating Pattern: The pattern reinforces the product identification.

Layered: The design elements create a sense of depth of information.

Split Image: The front of the packaging design is split in such a way that when the products are positioned next to one another on shelf they complete a design or create a pattern.

Action: The imagery communicates the interactive nature of the product.

Subtle: The design suggests a personality using a soft, low-contrast style.

Breakout: The concept is a complete departure from what is expected from the category or product.

Signature: The individuality of the design is communicated through a typographic signature, stamp, or date of authenticity.

**Lindsay Olives
Redesign Sketches**
Client: Lindsay Olives
Design Firm:
Addis Design
Creative Director:
Steven Addis
Designer:
Debbie Smith

Initial concept
sketches explore
botanical drawings,
old-fashioned
fruit crate art, and
graphics that visually
express the brand's
heritage.

Visual Hierarchy

The hierarchy of information—how the packaging design is to be read—must be considered in this phase. The position of the brand name relative to the name of the manufacturer and the placement of the flavor, variety, and product benefits copy all weigh in what become important communication elements of the packaging design. What the consumer reads first, second, and third are all determined by the layout. The layout for the front panel creates the order for reading the information. The size, color, positioning, and relationship of the design elements affect how the consumers' eyes move across the primary display panel and how they understand the importance and relevance of all of the information provided. On any given packaging design, there may be several levels of communication. For example, there may be an umbrella brand with a sub-brand, or there may be a product that is co-branded.

The design distinctions between multiple products in a line need careful consideration. Product differentiations—whether for flavor, variety, scent, or ingredient—must be clear and easy for the consumer to distinguish. Maintaining the hierarchy of information consistently while using distinct shapes, colors, icons, and graphic imagery is the most common means to differentiate products within a line extension. Consumer confusion caused by an inability to differentiate between similar products in a line can seriously devalue a brand and contribute to loss of future sales.

PHASE 2

copy can reflect the mood on the pkg

Original ⚫
Oh! you never thought a cracker could taste so good and also be good for you!

Ranch: ➰
Yummmy! Lip-smacking savory Ranch crackers which tastes great and is also good for

Honey Sesame Smile crackers t so good as for you, have to you on

Kashi TLC Crackers
Client:
Kashi Company
Design Firm:
Addis Design
Designer/
Creative
Director:
Joanne Hom

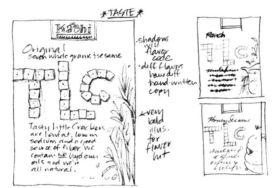

Addis Design's concept development for Kashi TLC Crackers focused on capturing the playfulness, healthy benefits, and taste appeal of the product. The initial design sketches demonstrate a whimsical personality that would capture consumer attention on shelf. The rendering styles depict different design strategies, but all of them make you smile. The final design direction gives the product star status with the combined use of lighthearted photography and illustration. The packaging design breaks the category with its distinctively fun approach to healthy snacking.

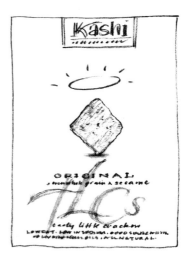

PHASE 2 The size relationship and hierarchy of information should be checked to make sure the designs read accurately. Asking questions such as, What does the eye read first, second, and third? provides the designer with answers to whether the design communicates as intended. There should be logical movement of the eye when scanning a packaging design. Since most people see an image before they read words, if there is a photograph or another image on a packaging design that is larger than the brand identity, that is what will be looked at first. The hierarchy of the design elements and how they are "read" can be altered by changing the elements, scale, positioning, or alignment in relation to other elements.

The key information on the preliminary display panel includes

- brand name(s) (may include corporate or parent brand name and sub-branding);
- product descriptor (what the product is);
- flavor, variety, fragrance, or product type;
- net weight (net wt.) or fluid ounce (fl.oz.) declaration;
- pack size or product count;
- romance copy or other product benefits.

The client may provide the text or copy for communicating product attributes, or the designer may be responsible for developing the copy. Copy information can be included in the initial sketches so that all of the pieces of communication are included. It is difficult to work in overlooked copy or other communication elements after designing a well-planned front panel.

DUMMY COPY

When the designer is not provided with all of the necessary copy in the early phase of the design process, they must "dummy" it in to give the appearance of the final layout. It is important to remember what "dummy" copy is as the design moves through the process. For example, designers made a fake recipe for the back panel of a stock pie-filling label. The design concept was selected as the final packaging design and went all the way to production and the retail shelf without anyone remembering that the recipe was made up.

Design Reviews and Presentations

The design reviews throughout Phase Two are where the initial concepts and preliminary ideas are presented, critiqued, and reviewed based on the strategic marketing objectives. In this review process initial layouts are tweaked, combined, or weeded out, leaving the most successful to be taken into the next phase of design development, in Phase Three.

During each subsequent phase of design, creative ideas are reviewed using different presentation methods. A wall critique is one method used to review designs. In this presentation the design concepts, sketches, swipes, and other reference material are taped on the wall and examined in their entirety. In a wall critique the panning of the entire visual area is a way to pull out designs that immediately attract the eye. Size relationships, typographic styles, contrasts, colors, graphic elements, symbols, and the cropping of photographs and illustrations are all critiqued in depth.

In all design presentations there should be an open dialogue regarding design concepts. Critiques should focus on the concepts and how a design could have greater impact, how others can be improved or modified, and which design concepts are weak and should be disregarded. The purpose of a design critique is to improve the creative work with the goal of creating a marketable solution that meets the client's needs.

Sherwin-Williams
Client:
Sherwin-Williams,
Adam Chafe/Vice
President Marketing
Consumer Division
Design Firm:
Group 4
Product Design
Director: Bob Bruno

Ideas should be presented in an organized format. Thumbnails and initial layouts should be positioned neatly on paper and be clean and free of rips and wrinkles. Ideas should be sketched in a size that is easily viewed from a few feet back. Ideas ripped out of a sketchbook, drawn on a paper towel, or clipped from a newspaper are fine for personal use but are inappropriate for a group presentation. A strong presentation is one in which the designs are presented in a professional manner.

Often the review process takes place in a small setting, where the work is collected and critiqued without the designer present. In this case, as in all design scenarios, the work on paper must speak for itself. Designs must clearly communicate the designer's intention or concept in a format that does not need a verbal presentation. The use of call-outs or word descriptions to identify specific elements is a means to verbally communicate design intentions. Swipes of textured papers, colors, images, and type styles can be affixed to a layout to aid in the communication of a design concept.

PHASE 2

CASE STUDY

The design process is illustrated with hand-rendered sketches that are translated and developed as computer sketches. The selected design direction is refined, and the final imagery is photographically styled to perfection.

"As Addis Design describes [they] "distilled the Frulatté product positioning into the brand essence of 'happy body' and then brought that idea into tangible life in a way that disrupts category norms with a completely new standard of packaging".

Frulatté Design Development
(spread)
Client: Frulatté
Design Firm: Addis Design
Creative Director: Michael Roché, Joanne Hom
Designer: Joanne Hom

  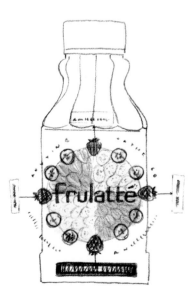

frula

naturally fresh smoothie

orange mango

monterey strawberry kiwi

frulatté
all natural fruit-blended beverage

naturally
fresh
smoothie

frulatté
cranberry
raspberry

flash pasteurized
to preserve freshness

orange mango

frulatté
naturally fresh smoothie

frulatte
orange-mango

PHASE 2

Throughout each presentation, clear articulation is important since both verbal and visual information can easily be misunderstood. Asking specific questions, listening carefully, and fielding feedback and criticisms can aid in the success of the communication process. With the goal of selling ideas, visuals should be clean, organized, well executed, and convey strong solutions and concepts in a presentable manner.

Do not throw away design sketches or concepts that did not made it past the first round of critiques. A concept that did not work for one assignment may be a possible solution for another project. Organization and file-management skills can help to keep work readily accessible.

SOURCING IMAGERY

Sourcing imagery illustration and/or photography to be used in packaging design are a significant responsibility. An awareness of and sensitivity to copyright and intellectual property laws is an important factor. The designer is responsible for sourcing and buying stock photography and/or illustration and establishing the usage terms, all factored into and dependent on a client's budget. Fees are affected by choice of imagery and its expected usage. The fee for an image used for a focus group or test market is different than that for a packaging design with regional, national, or international distribution. If the client's budget provides for it, the creation of proprietary (ownable) visuals can be achieved by hiring an illustrator or a photographer. In this case a contract of usage is critical. A total buyout is when the client wants complete ownership of the creative image or property. A budget that does not provide for the purchasing of preexisting creative property or the hiring of a creative artist means that the designer must develop any imagery used.

Lindsay Olives Redesign
Client: Lindsay Olives
Design Firm: Addis Design
Creative Director: Steven Addis
Designer: Debbie Smith

Old (left), Initial Color Sketch (middle), New (right). The redesign unified the brand's products and highlighted its authenticity.

PHASE 3: Design Development

The creative exploration from Phase Two is narrowed down to strategic directions that move into the design development of Phase Three. The core of the design process happens here, where a selected number of creative directions are developed with concepts becoming more refined.

With the brand identities that were initially rough sketches resolved further, their impact becomes a critical component to the narrowing-down process. Type choice (style, font, and use of upper- or lowercase letters), graphic treatment (outlines, drop shadows), alignment (centered, justified, flush left), kerning, ligatures, and word spacing are all explored in detail. A number of variations of each brand identity are developed during this phase. Typefaces are resolved with the goal of creating a more distinct and "ownable" brand identity.

Graphic devices such as banners, bands, windows, waves, characters, symbols, icons, and patterns are defined as to their relevance to the packaging design concept. These may be used with the logotype as a means of creating a more distinguishable brand identity or as another specific visual communication tool elsewhere on the packaging design. Each element should be purposeful and not merely decorative, and its use should be determined by how it supports the design strategy.

At this stage in the process the use of photography or illustration is determined. Where design concepts incorporate a photographic image, the use of stock photography or creating the photograph with a digital camera is the best way to proceed. Since the design concept may not be selected to go beyond this stage, it is unwise to spend the money on a photographer to create a custom image. The same holds true for illustration. Unless the client's budget allows for the hiring of an illustrator at this phase, an illustration can be created by hand or borrowed from stock.

It is important that when a design concept uses a "temporary" image, the client be informed that the image is a placeholder and intended solely as a means of expressing a concept. If the client selects this design concept as one of the final solutions, the hiring of a photographer or illustrator or the purchase of stock imagery will be required.

Choice is essential in this phase. More than one option for logotype, imagery, and color for any design concept should be developed as well as a variety of concepts that focus on different ways to communicate a chosen strategy. Simply modifying the same design concept through changes in layout and brand identities is not enough. The designs must clearly reflect the marketing objectives, and there are many ways to achieve this. The specific elements of each design must communicate as a whole: the hierarchy, color, imagery, layout, and structure must all read properly.

CASE STUDY

Vicky Arzano of Toast explains that "both clients and consumers have become more visually sophisticated over the years. Technology has enabled the designer to present concepts to a degree of finish that is very close to the final product. Adobe Photoshop has now replaced markers as the tool for creating concept images. There still needs to be a strong idea and getting there can be a lot more labor, intensive than a few strokes of a marker and some explanation. The designer needs to acquire a whole new set of skills—retoucher, illustrator, and techno-geek to get the message across."

Toast's concept development process included the use of retro ethnic imagery to conjur up the agricultural heyday of the fruit crate art era and suggest "fresh from the farm" picked fruit. Additional concepts continue to express the full, flavor, freshness of oranges while exploring the quenching, premium quality of the product.

Images for Comping
Some of the imagery used was not copyright free and would either have to be recreated or the rights negoiated and cleared if the client had picked this concept.

Add gradations to background for glow effect.

Digital photo of orange half. Retouch out distracting white center.

Lady lifted from fruit crate lable

Rows of orange trees from fruit crate label.

Oranges from an old advertisement.

Finished concept

IMPORTANT: Had the client chosen this design all art that is not copyright free would have to be recreated.

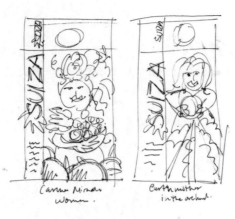

**Suiza Premium
Redesign**
Client:
Morningstar Foods
Design Firm:
Toast
Designer:
Victoria Arzano

PHASE 3

All primary and secondary copy and graphics for the primary display panel (PDP) are resolved further, and the designs for the top, bottom, back, and sides of the packaging design are developed. Final copy requirements for the product are incorporated. Flavor descriptors, varieties, product names, and romance copy (that which creates the story or description for the product) are incorporated into the design. Initial positioning and layout of the legal requirements of weight, volume, or product count are added to the front panel. Depending on the type of product, mandatory requirements such as nutrition information, ingredients, warnings, and directions are positioned in the design at this point or during the final phase.

Color options are explored, with particular emphasis on selecting the appropriate color palette for the visual communication of the product's message.

Color considerations during Phase Three include:

- color in relation to the competition;
- color as a means of clearly identifying the varieties in the product line;
- color to communicate a specific personality, feature, or theme;
- color to communicate flavor, scent, or season.

Baby Magic
Client: Playtex Products Inc.
Design Firm: R.Bird
Art Director: Richard Bird,
Creative Director: Joseph Favata

Old packaging design (top left and top right); New packaging design with tapered bottle and redesigned brand identity (bottom).

General Guidelines for Net Weight or Product Contents Copy

The net weight copy must be placed on the bottom half of the front, or primary display panel, of the packaging design. The legal font size is determined by guidelines outlined in the Food and Drug Administration's Packaging and Labeling Guidelines (www.fda.gov). For initial packaging designs, the general rule is that the height of the letters should be no less than 3 millimeters and the baseline should be no less than 3 millimeters from the sides or bottom of the primary display panel.

The positioning of the weight content copy should be consistent with the overall design layout. In general, if the grid of the PDP is primarily a centered format, then the net weight should be centered as well. If the general design format is flush left, then the copy should be fitted accordingly. There are times when it is preferable to stack the copy on two lines and tuck it to the right or left of the layout. The design and placement of this copy should not be an afterthought or randomly placed but as intentional as the rest of the visual elements.

PRINTING FOR PRESENTATION

The rule of thumb for initial presentations is that what the client sees is what they think they will get. Never try to talk the client through what the "real" imagery or color will be. Whatever is presented to a client is what they think the finished design will look like. If the printer used for a Phase Three presentation does not accurately reproduce the colors intended, then an alternative means of printing the packaging design must be determined.

Comprehensives

Comps are three-dimensional models or prototypes that provide the designer and the marketer with a realistic representation of the final printed packaging design. These mock-ups are full-scale simulations of the packaging design. Comps allow the designer to apply the brand identity and all of the other design elements effectively around all the sides of the packaging. Designers use comps to help themselves and their client visualize the packaging design in three-dimensional form. Comps can be created during any phase of the design process, but they are essential in Phase Three as a tool for review and approval.

The importance of a flawlessly assembled comp cannot be overstressed. A comp should be the very best presentation of how the finished packaging design will look—an exact replica of the printed package. The precision that is achieved in the craft of comp assembly is often far better than what will ever be reproduced in mass quantity.

PHASE 3

With this in mind, the designer must be a perfectionist with the measurements of the structure, the positioning of all of the elements, and the quality of printing when creating a comp.

In the comp, three-dimensional format size relationships and positioning of graphic elements can be assessed and adjusted. Graphics and text can be positioned close to the edges of the page on a two-dimensional surface and still be legible. On a three-dimensional structure, a can for example, there is a certain width that faces the consumer. Anything beyond this width is out of the focal point. Additionally, in three-dimensional design the layout and positioning is affected by printing and production limitations such as the distance from folds, scores, and cuts on a folding carton. Graphics that appear successful on a two-dimensional surface may look soft and recessive on a three-dimensional structure, in comparison to competitive products, or in the general retail environment. Comps can be revised, modified, or discarded as the focus moves to narrow the choices of marketable solutions.

Since comps provide a realistic view of the final printed design, they are often used in consumer research; are photographed for advertising, television, and promotional materials; and are often displayed at sales meetings and trade events. Television commercials and print advertisements generally use a comp or mock-up of the original packaging design. Referred to as "beauty" or "hero" packaging design, they present the design with the most immediately identifiable attributes of the front panel. The brand identity, key front panel graphics, and the consumer touch points remain on the packaging design; all other extenuating elements, such as the net weight and secondary copy and elements, are removed.

There are many businesses that support the design development process through comp or prototype design, development, and production. Capabilities may include injection molding, screen printing, printing high-resolution digital files, embossing, foil stamping, or creating typographic transfers.

In general, agreed-upon deadlines determine when each phase of the process ends. Although designs can be tweaked forever, sometimes they just have to be finished to meet the deadline. Perfectionism is a character trait of good designers, and it is difficult to look at a design and decide that it is complete. Knowing when a design is as close to perfect as possible comes with experience and a keenly developed sense of intuition. The goal of Phase Three is to create a number of tightly refined design solutions that meet the specific strategy. Preferred designs are chosen to move forward and become the final packaging design.

Packaging Design Comps

Fuzion (top)
Designer:
Jason Lombardo/FIT
(Fashion Institute of
Technology)

Pisces (middle)
Pro Grade (bottom)
Designer:
Robert Ludemann/
FIT (Fashion Institute
of Technology)

The brand identity
and all other graphic
elements are
effectively applied
to these packaging
structures.

PHASE 3

**Discovery
Channel
Retail
Program**
Client:
Discovery
Channel
Design Firm:
Parham
Santana
Creative
Director:
John Parham
Senior Art
Director:
Dave Wang
Designer:
Emily Pak

The family-
oriented retail
experience was
defined through
a comprehensive
packaging and
merchandising
program
for the
Discovery
Channel
Stores.

Research

Examination of the "equity" or valuable elements of the packaging design concepts are fully explored in Phase Three. Consider what Malcolm Gladwell refers to in his book *Blink* as the two seconds it takes to make an initial judgment or a snap decision—that is about how long it takes for the average consumer to "get" the communication of a packaging design in the retail environment.

Consumer research in this phase can help to assess the value of the design elements and how they contribute to the brand's equity. Research may also include in-store audits, market tests, focus groups, or other tools used to determine how the packaging designs connect with the target consumer. Physically placing the comp or "mock-up" of the packaging design in its retail environment is another approach to assessing the design's impact. Digital planograms of a product category or shelf set can be another way to determine if the design concept is successfully breaking out from competitors.

Research in Phase Three can help to:

- observe the strengths and weaknesses of the competition;
- explore new inspiration and approaches for design concepts;
- examine the consumer's response.

In Phase Three it is important for all of the design elements to be organized and layered appropriately in digital files, and production issues are taken into consideration. This is the time to check with suppliers and related production support to ensure that the developing design concepts are producible.

The tight development of a range of distinct brand personalities for the product during Phase Three makes it is easier to determine which ones truly meet all aspects of the clients marketing objectives. Some concepts may be too "far out," meaning they meet the design objectives but stretch the traditional design realm of the category, the product perception, or the client's initial goals. Some concepts may be considered conservative. These designs meet the design objectives and do not risk anything—they are straightforward and direct. Understanding the client's expectations helps to guide the outcome of this process.

PHASE 4: Final Design Refinement

Each and every design element in the final chosen design concept undergoes a refinement process in this concluding design phase. Refinement may be directed by client preference or mutually agreed-upon decisions regarding color, typographic treatment, or graphic imagery. The focus is to resolve the design so that each element serves a specific function and clearly communicates the intended objective.

The final brand identity development is given very careful attention. The shapes of the letterforms are consistently balanced, letters and words are properly organized, and kerning, ligatures, and outlines are all refined. Structural dimensions, secondary copy layout and positioning, colors, graphic imagery, and each design element are all reviewed. All copy, including mandatory copy, is checked for correctly spelled words. All legal considerations are checked by the design team and approved by the client's legal representative as necessary. Slight variations of the final solution, based on one design direction, may be developed into a few final comprehensives for the final presentation.

Physically stepping away from the design; making sure that everything comes together to make a strong, legible, clear, and positive impression; and making certain that the design clearly communicates the product's personality through the imagery, color, typography, and layout are part of the final check. The final packaging design should be an attention grabber and clearly resolve the marketing objective.

Research indicates that 85 percent of the products that get touched get picked up and ultimately sold. As Marcus Hewitt, Managing Partner and Chief Creative Officer of Sterling Brands states, "We talk about the 'brand in the hand'—consumers need to be drawn to a brand's range of products but will hopefully pick up one. This is when the more intimate connection is made and when the packaging design needs to work in more subtle ways to communicate its value."

Billboard

In packaging design the term *billboard* refers to the appearance of a brand of products that form a strong communication presence together. Creating a billboard is a way for a brand to leverage its shelf presence by positioning packaging designs with a brand or brand family together for greater shelf impact. The consistency of a brand's packaging design—through structural orientation, graphic layout, and brand identity on the shelf—creates the foundation for an effective billboard.

THE IMPACT OF BILLBOARDING

Why would we use a term like *billboard* when we're referring to a package that might be just a few inches high?

It is important to remember that the packaging designs being created are not presented to consumers individually. Although designers focus on the particulars of the lovingly crafted boxes, tubes, jars, and bottles, they are ultimately jammed into crowded shelves right next to their competitors'. The trick is to use the necessity of multiples as a design advantage. This is achieved through repetition, where designs are multiplied and have greater impact.

Just as designers can make one packaging design stand out through the distinctive use of structure, graphics, and color, the same techniques can be applied when products are grouped with duplicates or varietals. This is *billboarding*.

Perrier, and more recently Pom, achieved their billboarding structurally. The graphics actually don't matter too much. These brands are distinctive because of the bottle shape. Arizona Iced Tea first used shrink-film labels to totally cover their bottles, and their billboard effect was significant.

Of course, the brand mark can create a billboard as well. Consider Jif preserves or the classic Oxo bouillon X, which becomes the entire packaging design. Repeated use of a heart-shaped window for Post ties together a diverse range of cereals. Boxes are great when it comes to graphic repetition. Fruit juice tetra packs are a gift to designers when it comes to having the design link from one packaging to another.

In billboarding the critical link is often color. Think of Campbell's red-and-white soups or Pepperidge Farm's emphasis on white packs. Ronzoni's line of pastas creates a stunning wall of blue. Sometimes removing elements can make a brand stand out: Absolut and more recently Apple use the minimal approach to stand out from the crowd. This highlights the other key to billboarding: Keep it simple. Billboarding can be thought of as volume—you can turn it up to get attention or turn it down to draw someone in. Billboarding is a means, but it's not the end. The "end" is creating a brand that resonates with old and new consumers.

Marcus Hewitt, Managing Partner and Chief Creative Officer,
Sterling Brands

PHASE 4   Phase Four should end with the client approval of the final comp. Often the client keeps the final comps of the packaging design to present at a board meeting, a sales meeting, or to other members of the approval team. It is wise to make a few extra final comps for this purpose. The design team should keep one final comp in case further refinements or revisions are requested. In addition, since client-designer communication does not always take place in person, having a copy of what the client has in hand enables both parties to communicate via telephone and visually refer to the same design.

If the design proposal places responsibility for outsourcing the printers, suppliers (bottles, caps, closures), or other vendors (embossers, engravers) on the design team, it is at this time that final production quotes from vendors are submitted, reviewed, negotiated, and approved.

PHASE 5: Pre-Production and Digital Mechanicals

Getting the final approved packaging design ready for production is the next step and the designer or design firm may be responsible for preparing the final production files. This is made easier if all of the design files have been well organized throughout the process so they can be easily identified and if documents reflect the most current version of the approved design.

When the project is given final approval by the client, all electronic files are configured accordingly and the job is ready to be passed off to a production professional and ultimately submitted to the printer (See Chapter 9: Planning for Production). The last responsibility of the designer may be to attend the first press check, where the designer meets with the printer on-site to review the specifications (specs) of the job and to oversee the first print run to establish quality standards. Once the press check is approved the job is complete.

Production Checklist

Final preparation of material for print production requires that the following be provided to the printer:

- digital mechanical file(s);
- all fonts;
- color proof(s);
- all high-resolution image files;
- color specifications (especially spot colors);
- indications and separations of layers;
- confirmation that all colors will reproduce in the correct printing process;
- a listing of the number of colors;
- specification of high-gloss coating, uv matte coating, or combination;
- specification of die cuts and/or windows;
- specification of other special finishing techniques.

Key Points about the Design Process

✓ "Paint a picture" of the strategic objectives through the marketing brief.

✓ Understand the long-term strategic objectives for a product or brand.

✓ Manage time appropriately.

✓ Ask pertinent questions up front.

✓ Analyze the product and category characteristics.

✓ Involve all the stakeholders.

✓ Follow a sequential design process.

✓ Maintain visual hierarchy.

✓ Consider environmentally sound design options.

✓ Keep the consumer in mind at all times.

✓ Assess the potential design solutions as they communicate within the retail environment.

✓ Plan for production.

✓ Be able to defend, define, and provide a rationale for design concepts.

✓ Present flawless comps.

11 CONSIDERING THE ENVIRONMENT

The Three "R's"

The three "R's"—Reduce, Reuse, and Recycle—is a phrase that characterizes our society's long-standing concerns over manufacturing and production waste and their effects on the environment. Environmental concerns and the efforts to pursue the principles of turning waste back into raw materials dates back at least three centuries. Susan Strasser, in her book *Waste and Want: A Social History of Trash Recycling* details how recycling became inherent to production in various industries, central to the distribution of consumer goods, and an important habit of daily life.

The concept of recycling during the 1960s focused on reclamation and this became the catch word of the times. During the early 1970s an environmental movement promoted the separate collection of certain kinds of trash to encourage reuse in manufacturing. The packaging industry came under the spotlight during the 1970s oil crisis, in which energy conservation was mandated and resulted in part in reduced packaging. Lighter packages reduced not only the amount of resources used in manufacturing but also cut energy used in transportation, shipping more products that weighed less.

THE RECYCLING SYMBOL

In 1970, the year of the first Earth Day, the Container Corporation of America, at the time the nation's largest producer of recycled paperboard, sponsored a contest for a design that symbolized the recycling process. The design was to appear on the company's recycled paperboard products.

Gary Anderson, a senior at the University of Southern California, won the contest, judged at the 1970 International Design Conference, in Aspen, Colorado. His design, three chasing arrows, was based on nineteenth-century mathematician August Ferdinand Mobius's discovery that a strip of paper twisted once over and joined at the tips formed a continuous single-edged one-sided surface. Thus the recycling symbol is called a Mobius loop. The arrows represent collection, processing, and usage of materials. (Source: American Forest and Pulp Association)

The Resource Conservation and Recovery Act (RCRA) was passed in October 1976 with goals that included the following:

■ Reduce waste and increase the efficient and sustainable use of resources.
■ Prevent exposure to humans and ecosystems from the use of hazardous chemicals.
■ Manage waste and clean up chemical releases in a safe, environmentally sound manner.

During the 1980s and 1990s environmental concerns focused on the growing waste problem predicated on our throwaway society. Solid waste was being generated with little consideration of how to dispose of it. Recycling and preventing used consumer goods and packaging materials from becoming solid waste became an issue with the rising costs of disposal and increasing environmental activism.

Packaging materials that can be recycled include paper, paperboard, wood, glass, plastic, aluminum, and steel. These materials are used for:

■ Primary packaging (handled by the consumer)

- Secondary packaging (larger boxes, cases, outer structures used for shipping and distribution)
- Transport packaging (wooden pallets, boards, paper, and plastic wrappings used for large loads)

The three "R's" have become part of our consumer mantra. From a packaging perspective, their employment means that the production process, from product development to packaging design, production, and distribution, must be assessed.

Increased societal concern has consumer products companies and the packaging industry continually assessing what effect their activities have on the environment. In response they have provided "greener" products and packaging that are better for the environment. However, the model of product design and packaging design must be changed so there is a *closed* loop of return, reuse and recyclability.

Packaging and Life-Cycle Assessment

The packaging industry, along with others, has begun to adopt ways to assess their practices in relation to the environment. Life-Cycle Assessment (LCA) is one of the objective processes used to evaluate the environmental burdens associated with a product, process, or activity. The LCA process identifies energy and materials used and wastes released into the environment, and evaluates and implements opportunities to apply environmental improvements.

The current terminology *cradle-to-grave* refers to the life-cycle assessment model of many products and packaging. Cradle-to-grave begins with the gathering of raw materials from the earth to create the product and ends at the point when all materials are returned to the earth.

The LCA Process

- Evaluates all stages of a product's life from the perspective that they are interdependent, meaning that one operation leads to the next;
- Enables the estimation of the cumulative environmental impact resulting from all stages in the product life cycle, often including those not considered in more traditional analyses (e.g., raw material extraction, material transportation, ultimate product disposal, etc.);
- Provides a comprehensive view of the environmental aspects of the product or process and a more accurate picture of the true environmental trade-offs in product selection.

Environmental Factors

Packaging design is forced to meet the conflicting objectives of manufacturing, marketing, and the demands of the consumer. The compromise comes between manufacturers of consumer goods, producers of packaging and packaging materials, and the retailer, with all parties wanting to deliver a product successfully to the consumer—economically and efficiently. The type and amount of packaging needed to ensure the safety of the product is weighed against what will likely become waste after product use or consumption.

The many factors that affect environmental choices as they relate to packaging design and packaging materials are:

- Demands of the product;
- Demands of the production process;
- Distribution/transportation system;
- Storage (warehouse, retail, home);
- Corporate (responsibility) policy of both the goods manufacturer and the packaging and packaging materials producers;
- Government regulations;
- Marketing;
- Retailer requirements;
- Consumer needs and wants.

Annie Chun's
The biodegradable bowl and recycled paperboard sleeve of this packaging design reflects a company that cares about the environment.

One way the packaging industry is tackling environmental issues is by working directly with consumer products companies on waste prevention through source reduction. The saving of natural resources in manufacturing by using recycled materials and developing new low-impact or environmentally sensitive materials is a means of source reduction. Packaging can play a significant role in this regard by being recyclable, taking up less space as waste, and being biodegradable at a faster rate in landfills or composting facilities.

Rolling Hills Organic Milk
Company:
Naturally Iowa

New material technologies being introduced into the mainstream consumer landscape are soon to become the norm rather than the exception. Polylactide polymer NatureWorks® PLA from Cargill Dow is derived from corn and breaks down in the commercial composting facility. Naturally Iowa packages milk in half-gallon PLA bottles, and its slogan, "We Milk the Cows and Grow the Bottles," is dedicated to organic farming practices.

BIOTA Colorado Spring Water
Company:
BIOTA Brands of America, Inc.
Designer:
David M. Zutler

BIOTA Brands of America, a PLAnet friendly company, introduced the world's first bottled water to be packaged in a commercially biodegradable plastic bottle made from a 100 percent renewable resource, corn.

Source Reduction

"Source reduction" is the practice of designing, manufacturing, purchasing, or using materials (such as products and packaging) in ways that reduce the amount or toxicity of trash created before they become municipal solid waste (MSW). Source reduction also refers to the reuse of products or materials. Reusing items is another way to stop waste at the source because it delays or prevents that item's entry in the waste collection and disposal system. Source reduction, including reuse, can help reduce waste disposal and handling costs because it avoids the costs of recycling, municipal composting, landfilling, and combustion. Source reduction also conserves resources and reduces pollution, including greenhouse gases that contribute to global warming.

Waste Management

Waste management and regulation are among the biggest issues today. On the one side is the question of the responsibility of manufacturers of goods and packaging and retailers in waste management. On the other side are issues of compliance enforcement, and whether it should be industry-led and self-regulated or enforced by the government on federal, state, and local levels.

The EPA's Office of Solid Waste (OSW) regulates household garbage and the solid and hazardous waste produced by industrial and manufacturing processes from "cradle-to-grave" under the 1976 Resource Conservation and Recovery Act (RCRA).

The OSW white paper on a vision for the future considered the following trends and future directions:

- pressures on natural resources will continue to increase;
- new technologies will change how resources are used and wasted;
- there will be a need for more sustainable use of resources;
- more chemicals will bring new risks;
- methods for measuring and managing chemical risks will improve;
- industry will consume and waste different types of materials;
- industries will be more efficient and less wasteful;
- waste will still be with us;
- the information revolution will continue;
- industries, individuals, and the environment will benefit from the information revolution;
- the global economy will be more highly integrated;
- environmental protections will need to be more internationalized;

- people will have more influence in environmental decisions;
- the size and cultural diversity of the U.S. population will continue to increase and will affect environmental decision making.

Europe's *Directive on Packaging and Packaging Waste*, issued in 1994, placed direct responsibility and specific packaging waste-reduction targets on all manufacturers, importers, and distributors of products on the EU market.

The EU's environmental objectives were to:

- reduce over packaging;
- eliminate certain dangerous materials from packaging;
- provide consumers with information;
- reduce the proportion of packaging waste going to landfill;
- increase recovery and recycling of packaging waste;
- put the burden of recovery and recycling on the producer.

To meet the goals of the United States Environmental Protection Agency (www.epa. gov/epaoswer/non-hw/muncpl/timeline_alt.htm), take-back schemes for product packaging have to be developed and implemented by manufacturers, importers, and distributors, or they have to join industry-driven nonprofit organizations that collect, sort, and recycle used packaging. The standard take-back program currently is the Green Dot Program; 21 European countries and Canada are on board.

A DESIGN CHALLENGE

As part of an initiative to investigate innovative solutions and strategies to eliminate or reduce waste and encourage a more integrated approach to the design of packaging, the U.S. Environmental Protection Agency (EPA), partnered with McDonough Braungart Design Chemistry (MBDC) on a design challenge. The goal was to develop more sustainable packaging services through the design of environmentally preferable packaging and the complementary systems needed for value recovery using cradle-to-cradle principles. (See www.mbdc.com/challenge.)

**Recycling
Sorting Facility**
Photo:
Nicole F. Smith,
Design & Source
Productions Inc.

Consumer recycling
coming into sorting
facility.

Sorted Cube
Photo:
Nicole F. Smith,
Design & Source
Productions Inc.

Once consumers'
recycling comes into
the facility, all
items are sorted by
hand, and divided
by plastic and color,
and then cubed.

Creating Change

In past decades packaging waste was not a factor for consumers in the purchasing decisions at the retail shelf, but came into play after goods were used at home and they had to consider the products' disposal. Consumers today are more environmentally aware of the role of packaging in product protection and in many cases will make purchasing decisions based on this factor alone. Raising awareness of the critical role of packaging helps to promote consumer responsibility for the environmental impact of products and their respective packages.

The packaging design industry must lead the charge in environmental responsibility, including encouraging manufacturers and marketers to:

- use environmentally sourced paper and printing such as recycled paper, tree-free paper, chlorine-free paper, papers printed with soy ink, and nontoxic toners;
- use digital printing, which avoids films and chemicals in the normal printing process;
- use tree-free products such as hemp, denim, old money, and materials that degrade back into a natural environmental form;

- reduce and eliminate the use of toxic chemicals such as dioxin that cause cancer, harm and kill wildlife, and pollute water;
- consider waste reduction within product life cycle from raw material acquisition (materials can be sustainable harvested, petroleum-free, and plant-based); material processing (materials can be chemical-free and unbleached); product manufacturing (manufacturing that avoids and reduces environmental pollution by reducing production of aerosol products); product use and consumption (reduction in the use of nonenvironmentally friendly products including aerosols and purchasing products with reduced packaging); and disposal (recycle, reuse, and refill).

Marketing and manufacturing should take a socially responsible stance on environmental concerns as follows:

- Consider using recycled materials from papers to plastics.
- Cut down on secondary packaging and over packaging.
- Make concentrated products, which mean less environmental impact on packaging and shipping.
- Consider the effects of shipping and transportation on the environment. Slower shipping reduces the greenhouse-gas emissions and is energy-efficient.
- Examine cost-benefit models for environmentally sensitive packaging and design for short- and long-term gains.

Recycled EVA Packaging
Photo:
Nicole F. Smith,
Design & Source
Productions Inc.

Molded packaging and trays made of Post-Industrial Recycled EVA (Ethyl Vinyl Acetate)

Key Points about the Environment

✓ Assess the processes used to evaluate the environmental burdens associated with a product, process, or activity.

✓ Consider the type and amount of packaging needed to ensure the safety of the product.

✓ Promote product after-use, waste prevention, and source reduction.

12 UNDERSTANDING LEGAL ISSUES

Understanding Legal Issues

Packaging design must conform to government legislation and regulatory standards. The country, state, and region in which the product is manufactured, packaged, transported, exported, imported, and sold regulate the legal requirements. Product labeling, including ingredients, nutrition information, product claims, bar code compliance, specific product structural and material compliance, and brand logo or trademark registry, are among the legal issues concerning packaging design.

Although the client is ultimately responsible for all legal issues, the designer must apply all of the legal requirements as they relate to the packaging design.

The scope of legal requirements as they apply to the packaging design serve to:

- Ensure that the product contents are represented clearly and truthfully;
- Provide protection for the contents under normal conditions (from handling and distribution to retail and use);
- Ensure that the packaging is constructed with materials that will not have an adverse affect on the product;
- Promote consideration of the environment;
- Support the communication of the product contents;
- Protect the consumer from false claims.

With the serious nature of these issues, no packaging design should go to market before a legal authority approves the final design. Local, state, federal, and global regulatory authorities can provide detailed guidelines as they relate to the specific consumer product or packaging design assignment.

Laws and Regulatory Agencies

In the United States there are labeling distinctions based on the contents of the packaging. The Food and Drug Administration (FDA) is the agency within the Department of Health and Human Services (HHS) responsible for the regulation of products comprising more than 25 percent of American consumer spending. Other government agencies that regulate labeling include the Bureau of Alcohol, Tobacco and Firearms (ATF), for alcohol and tobacco products, and the United States Department of Agriculture (USDA) for meat, poultry, and egg products.

Major components of the FDA include field compliance and several product review centers. Field staff responsibility includes surveillance and enforcement, inspection of manufacturing facilities, observation of marketing and promotional activities, and recommendation and implementation of enforcement actions. The FDA jurisdiction over labeling is very broad.

Manufacturers must satisfy FDA legal and regulatory requirements, interpretations, and policies in order to receive FDA clearance or approval to enter U.S. markets. The FDA guidelines serve to provide a framework for regulations on the labeling of food products, drugs—prescription, over-the-counter (OTC), and generic—and cosmetics. Label guidelines include specific information such as how the label should focus on prioritizing items useful to the majority of consumers and that labeling should communicate food safety, consumer health, and nutritional information, product use, handling and storage. These guidelines focus on providing the consumer with information to make informed and healthy purchasing decisions. See the guidance documents on the FDA comprehensive Web site (www.fda.gov).

General Labeling Requirements

- Labeling must be legible and comprehensible.
- Information on a label must be indelible.
- Labeling particulars must be written in the official language or languages of the location where the product is to be sold.
- The mock-up of the packaging design with any proposed changes must be submitted to the legal authority for the manufacturer.
- Labeling or packaging must comply with federal, state, and regulatory agency requirements.

FEDERAL GOVERNING
REGULATORY DEPARTMENTS, OFFICES, & BUREAUS
FOR PACKAGING & LABELING

EXECUTIVE BRANCH   LEGISLATIVE BRANCH   JUDICIAL BRANCH

Department of Agriculture (USDA)

Food Safety and Inspection Service
Food Safety and Inspection Service is responsible for labeling of meat and poultry.

Department of Commerce

Patent and Trademark Office

Consumer Products Safety Commission
The FDA does not have jurisdiction over many household products. The Consumer Product Safety Commission is responsible for issues related to household appliances, paint, and toys.

Department of Treasury

Alcohol, Tobacco, Tax and Trade Bureau (TTB)

Advertising Formulation and Labeling Division

Department of Health and Human Services

Food and Drug Administration

Federal Food, Drug and Cosmetic Act

All food and drug regulations including labeling of
Diluted Wines
Cider with Less Than 7% Alcohol
Dealcoholized Wine and Malt Beverages
Use of Alcohol in Synthetic Foods

Federal Hazardous Substances Labeling Act

Department of Justice

Bureau of Alcohol, Tobacco and Firearms

FEDERAL INDEPENDENT AGENCIES
FOR CONSUMER PROTECTION

Consumer Product Safety Commission   **Federal Trade Commission**
Regulates all advertising excluding prescription drugs and medical devices.
Bureau of Consumer Protection
Division of Advertising Practices
Division of Marketing Practices
International Division of Consumer Protection

In the United States, every food package must have a label in English, which must include:

- The name of the product (invented name, trademark, or name of manufacturer);
- The name and address of the manufacturer or distributor, or if the product is imported, the name and address of the importer and the name of the country in which the food was produced;
- The batch number, SKU number, or indication of where the food was produced;
- A list of the ingredients expressed in weight order;
- Where the food in the package has a minimum durable life of less than 2 years, a "use-by date" or a "date of packaging," and the minimum durable life;
- If the minimum durable life is less than 90 days, there must include a statement of the "conditions of storage required ensuring the minimum durable life";
- Contents by weight, volume, or number of doses;
- Expiration date;
- Instructions for proper use of the product, in particular:
  Dosage
  Method and frequency of administration
  Action to be taken if the product is not taken as prescribed
  Indication, if necessary, of the risks
- Special warnings such as:
  The effects on driving ability
  "Must be stored out of reach of children"
  User categories such as "Not for children or pregnant women"

Packages and their labels should enable consumers to obtain accurate information as to the quantity of the contents and should facilitate value comparisons. Government policies are declared to assist consumers and manufacturers in reaching these goals in the marketing of consumer goods. It is unlawful for any person engaged in packaging or labeling of any consumer commodity to distribute for commerce (other than a common carrier for hire, a contract carrier for hire, or a freight forwarder for hire) any packaged or labeled consumer commodity that does not conform to the provisions and regulations under the authority of the FDA. The guidelines outlined by the FDA cannot be construed to repeal, invalidate, or supersede the Federal Trade Commission Act or any statute defined as an antitrust Act; the Federal Food, Drug, and Cosmetic Act; or the Federal Hazardous Substances Labeling Act. FDA guidelines define specific requirements of Labeling; Placement, Form, and Contents of Statement of Quantity; Supplemental Statement of Quantity.

Excerpts from the FDA Food Labeling Guide

FDA FOOD LABELING GUIDE
CHAPTER - 1 GENERAL FOOD LABELING REQUIREMENTS
(See: www.cfsan.fda.gov/~dms/flg-1.html)

1. Where should label statements be placed on containers and packages?

There are two ways to label packages and containers:
a. Place all required label statements on the front label panel (the principal display panel or PDP), or
b. Place certain specified label statements on the principal display panel and other labeling on the information panel (the label panel immediately to the right of the principal display panel, as seen by the consumer facing the product).

2. What are the principal display panel and the alternate principal display panel?

The principal display panel, or PDP, is that portion of the package label that is most likely to be seen by the consumer at the time of purchase. Many containers are designed with two or more different surfaces that are suitable for display as the PDP. These are alternate principal display panels. 21 CFR 101.1

3. What label statements must appear on the principal display panel?

Place the statement of identity, or name of the food, and the net quantity statement, or amount of product, on the PDP and on the alternate PDP. The required type size and prominence are discussed in Chapters 2 and 3. 21 CFR 101.3(a) and 101.105(a)

Chapter 1 Answer to Questions 2 & 3
FDA Reference
21 CFR 101.1,
21 CFR 101.3(a) and
CFR 101.105(a)
Food and Drug Administration
Center for Food Safety and Applied Nutrition
A Food Labeling Guide
September, 1994
(Editorial revisions June, 1999)

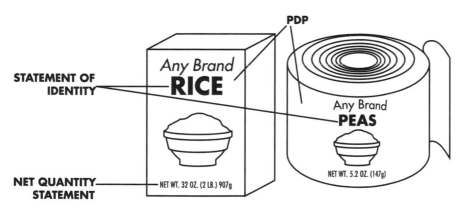

4. Which label panel is the information panel?

The information panel is the label panel immediately to the right of the PDP, as displayed to the consumer. If this panel is not usable, due to package design and construction, (e.g., folded flaps), then the information panel is the next label panel immediately to the right. 21 CFR 101.2(a)

5. What is information panel labeling?

The phrase "information panel labeling" refers to the label statements that are generally required to be placed together, without any intervening material, on the information panel, if such labeling does not appear on the PDP. These label statements include the name and address of the manufacturer, packer or distributor, the ingredient list, and nutrition labeling. 21 CFR 101.2(b) and (d)

Chapter 1 Answer
to Question 4
FDA Reference
21 CFR 101.2(a)
Food and Drug
Administration
Center for Food
Safety and Applied
Nutrition
A Food Labeling
Guide
September, 1994
(Editorial revisions
June, 1999)

Chapter 1 Answer
to Question 5
FDA Reference
21 CFR 101.2(b)
and (d)
Food and Drug
Administration
Center for Food
Safety and Applied
Nutrition
A Food Labeling
Guide
September, 1994
(Editorial revisions
June, 1999)

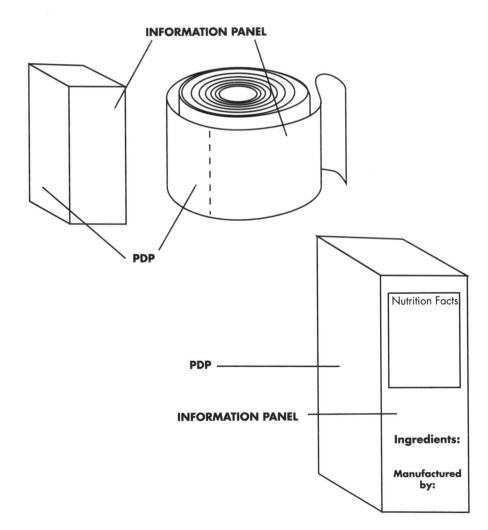

6. What type size, prominence, and conspicuousness are required?

For information panel labeling, use a print or type size that is prominent, conspicuous, and easy to read. Use letters that are at least one-sixteenth (1/16) inch in height based on the lowercase letter "o." The letters must not be more than three times as high as they are wide, and the lettering must contrast sufficiently with the background so as to be easy to read. Do not crowd required labeling with artwork or nonrequired labeling.

Smaller type sizes may be used for information panel labeling on very small food packages as discussed in 21 CFR 101.2(c).

Different type sizes are specified for the nutrition facts label.

The type-size requirements for the statement of identity and the net quantity statement are discussed in Chapters 2 and 3 of this booklet.
21 CFR 101.2(c) and 101.9(d)(1)(iii)

8. What name and address must be listed on the label?

Food labels must list:

1. Name and address of the manufacturer, packer, or distributor. Unless the name given is the actual manufacturer, it must be accompanied by a qualifying phrase, which states the firm's relation to the product, e.g., "manufactured for" or "distributed by." (Label-show manufacturer name and address);
2. Street address, if the firm name and address are not listed in a current city directory or telephone book;
3. City or town;
4. State (or country, if outside the United States); and
5. ZIP code (or mailing code used in countries other than the United States).

Chapter 1 Answer
to Question 6
FDA Reference
21 CFR 101.2(c)
and 101.9(d)(1)(iii)
Food and Drug
Administration
Center for Food
Safety and Applied
Nutrition
A Food Labeling
Guide
September, 1994
(Editorial revisions
June, 1999)

FDA FOOD LABELING GUIDE
CHAPTER 2 - NAME OF FOOD
(See: www.cfsan.fda.gov/~dms/flg-2.html)

1. What is the name of the food statement called, and where must it be placed?

The statement of identity is the name of the food. It must appear on the front label or principal display panel as well as any alternate principal display panel. 21 CFR 101.3

2. Should the statement of identity stand out? (Label Statement of Identity)

Use prominent print or type for the statement of identity. It shall be in bold type. The type size must be reasonably related to the most prominent printed matter on the front panel and should be one of the most important features on the principal display panel. Generally this is considered to be at least 1/2 the size of the largest print on the label. 21 CFR 101.3(d)

1. What name should be used as the statement of identity?
   The common or usual name of the food, if the food has one, should be used as the statement of identity. If there is none, then an appropriate descriptive name that is not misleading should be used. 21 CFR 101.3(b)

2. Where should the statement of identity be placed on the label?
   Place the statement of identity in lines generally parallel to the base of the package. 21 CFR 101.3(d)

3. When are fanciful names permitted as the statement of identity? (Label Fanciful Names)
   When the nature of the food is obvious, a fanciful name commonly used and understood by the public may be used. 21 CFR 101.3(b)(3)

4. Is it necessary to use the common or usual name instead of a new name?
   The common or usual name must be used for a food if it has one. It would be considered misleading to label a food that has an established name with a new name. If the food is subject to a standard of identity, it must bear the name specified in the standard. 21 CFR 101.3(b)(2)

FDA FOOD GUIDELINES
CHAPTER 3 - NET QUANTITY OF CONTENTS STATEMENTS
(See: www.cfsan.fda.gov/~dms/flg-3.html)

1. What is the net quantity of contents?

The net quantity of contents (net quantity statement) is the statement on the label that provides the amount of food in the container or package.
21 CFR 101.105(a)

4. Why is it necessary to calculate the area of the principal display panel?

The area of the principal display panel (calculated in square inches or square centimeters) determines the minimum type size that is permitted for the net quantity statement (see next question). Calculate the area of the principal display panel as follows: the area of a rectangular or square principal display panel on a carton is the height multiplied by the width (both in inches or both in centimeters).

To calculate the area of the principal display panel for a cylindrical container, multiply 40 percent of the height by the circumference.

Chapter 3 Answer to Question 4
FDA Reference 21 CFR 101.105 and 101.15
Food and Drug Administration Center for Food Safety and Applied Nutrition
A Food Labeling Guide
September, 1994 (Editorial revisions June, 1999)

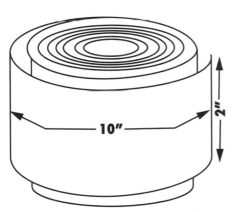

10" x 2" - 20 sq. in.
Area of PDP = 20 sq. in. x 40%
= 8 sq. in.

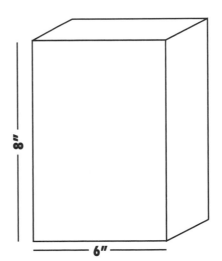

Area of PDP = 6" x 8" = 48 sq. in.

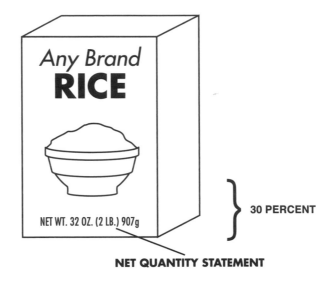

30 PERCENT

NET QUANTITY STATEMENT

Chapter 3 Answer
to Question 6
FDA Reference 21
CFR 101.105
Food and Drug
Administration
Center for Food
Safety and Applied
Nutrition
A Food Labeling
Guide
September, 1994
(Editorial revisions
June, 1999)

6. What are the conspicuousness and prominence requirements for net quantity statements?

Choose a print style that is prominent, conspicuous, and easy to read. The letters must not be more than three times as high as they are wide, and lettering must contrast sufficiently with the background to be easy to read. Do not crowd the net quantity statement with artwork or other labeling (minimum separation requirements are specified in the regulation). 21 CFR 101.105 and 101.15

FDA CHAPTER 4|IV INGREDIENT LIST

3. Where is the ingredient list placed on the label?

The ingredient list is placed on the same label panel as the name and address of the manufacturer, packer, or distributor. This may be either the information panel or the principal display panel. It may be before or after the nutrition label and the name and address of the manufacturer, packer, or distributor. 21 CFR 101.4(a)

An FDA guideline for commodity regulations does not:

- authorize any limitation on the size, shape, weight or mass, dimensions, or number of packages that should be used to enclose any commodity;
- regulate the placement upon any package of a retail sale price;
- require, in the listing of ingredients, that any trade secret be divulged.

FDA Additional Points

- Packages and their labels should enable consumers to obtain accurate information as to the quantity of the contents and should facilitate value comparisons. The policy of Congress is declared to assist consumers and manufacturers in reaching these goals in the marketing of consumer goods.
- It is unlawful for any person engaged in packaging or labeling of any consumer commodity to distribute for commerce (other than a common carrier for hire, a contract carrier for hire, or a freight forwarder for hire) any packaged or labeled consumer commodity that does not conform to the provisions and regulations under the authority of the FDA.
- The guidelines outlined by the FDA cannot be construed to repeal, invalidate, or supersede the Federal Trade Commission Act or any statute defined as an antitrust Act; the Federal Food, Drug, and Cosmetic Act; or the Federal Hazardous Substances Labeling Act.
- FDA guidelines define specific requirements of Labeling; Placement, Form, and Contents of Statement of Quantity; Supplemental Statement of Quantity.

FDA Terminology

Label: Any written, printed, or graphic matter affixed to any consumer commodity or affixed to or appearing upon a package containing any consumer commodity.

Commerce: Commerce between any State, the District of Columbia, the Commonwealth of Puerto Rico, or any territory or possession of the United States, and any place outside thereof, and commerce within the District of Columbia or within any territory or possession of the United States not organized with a legislative body, but shall not include exports to foreign countries.

Consumer commodity: Any food, drug, device, or cosmetic and any other article, product, or commodity of any kind or class that is customarily produced or distributed for sale through retail sales agencies for consumption by individuals, or use by individuals for purposes of personal care or in the performance of services ordinarily rendered within the household, and that usually is consumed or expended in the course of such consumption or use. Such term does not include:

- any meat or meat product, poultry or poultry product, or tobacco or tobacco product;
- any commodity subject to packaging or labeling requirements imposed by the Secretary of Agriculture pursuant to the Federal Insecticide, Fungicide, and Rodenticide Act or the Virus-Serum-Toxin Act;
- any drug subject to the provisions of the Federal Food, Drug, and Cosmetic Act;

- any beverage subject to or complying with packaging or labeling requirements imposed under the Federal Alcohol Administration Act;
- any commodity subject to the provisions of the Federal Seed Act.

Package: Any container or wrapping in which any consumer commodity is enclosed for use in the delivery or display of that consumer commodity to retail purchasers, but does not include shipping containers or wrappings used solely for the transportation of any consumer commodity in bulk or in quantity to manufacturers, packers, or processors, or to wholesale or retail distributors thereof; shipping containers or outer wrappings used by retailers to ship or deliver any commodity to retail customers if such containers and wrappings bear no printed matter pertaining to any particular commodity.

Principal display panel: That part of a label that is most likely to be displayed, presented, shown, or examined under normal and customary conditions of display for retail sale.

Federal regulatory organizations should be contacted for exact legal guidance regarding food, drug, cosmetic labeling. The Fair Packaging and Labeling Act Title 15|Commerce and Trade Chapter 39|Fair Packaging and Labeling Program provides more detailed information regarding cosmetics and over-the-counter labeling and claims, hair dyes, color additives, warning labels, ingredient labels, and more.

Intellectual Property Rights

Trademark

The brand name, logo, shape, color, and symbol or any combination of elements can either individually or collectively be considered a trademark. A trademark is used as the means of differentiating goods or services in commerce. The trademark indicates the source of the goods and can be used as a means of protecting its identity (if distinguishable). An initial trademark search on the Internet is a preliminary means of determining name use. Ultimately a legal expert should conduct a search before the design process begins. Trademark registration can help to prevent infringement.

Legally a trademark does not have to be registered. There is no fail-safe way to protect a trademark, however, registering a design or mark (it must be distinctive) can be used as a means of protecting a design from infringement and can be used in a court of law.

Copyright

A copyright protects original works from being copied. Manuscripts, advertising copy, packaging design copy, books, reports, images, and music can all obtain copyright protection. In packaging design, the ownership of artwork and design reside in the person or company that paid or retained for the design services (unless otherwise specified in writing). See www.copyright.gov/register to learn more about how to register a copyright.

Patents

Patents serve to protect an invention for 20 years. The critical point is that patent protection is available only if the owner can prove that the product, process, or business method is new and unique from anything else. There are utility patents that protect inventions such as machines, formulas, processes, and methods and design patents that protect industrial-design-related inventions. Patents do not have to be produced to be protected; therefore, a patent search would identify competitive patent applications. See the United States Patent and Trademark Office Web site at www.uspto.gov/web/patents/howtopat.htm to learn more about how to apply for a patent.

Registered Designs

A registered design is a way of protecting the outward appearance or design of product packaging. Registration can apply to a shape, ornament, graphic treatment (rendering, pattern, character), or configuration. The registration applies only to the actual visual appearance when in use. See the United States Patent and Trademark Office Web site at www.uspto.gov/web/offices/pac/design/toc.html to learn more about how to file a design patent application.

Trade Secrets and Confidentiality

The business of product development and packaging design is a highly competitive process. Trade secrets are extremely confidential and therefore protected by companies. Among the many forms of trade secrets are product development, marketing and merchandising plans, materials sources, supplier lists, general terms and prices, processes, and formulas. Client communications, design projects, and marketing plans should never be revealed or discussed outside of the company. Confidentiality is of utmost importance in a designer-client relationship. Both design firms and designers are often asked to sign legally binding confidentiality agreements to assure that classified information remains secret.

UNDERSTANDING INTELLECTUAL PROPERTY

It is important for clients to understand how intellectual property fits within their business and how to maximize its value to them. A simple trademark registration takes a few weeks to prepare and about a year to bring to conclusion. Patent filings take at least several weeks, often months, and usually two or more years to complete. Development of an intellectual property program takes several months and enforcement continues indefinitely. Litigations take from several months to several years. There are both rights and risks associated with these areas.

Robert Hanlon, Attorney, Senior Trademark and Copyright Partner in the Intellectual Property Group, New York Office of Alston & Bird LLP.

Counterfeiting and Packaging Design

A global problem for packaging designs, brand designs, and consumer products is counterfeiting. Knock-off or copy-cat products account for a significant percentage of all products marketed throughout the world. The availability and sophistication of digital technology has enabled thieves to create realistic replicas of virtually any product. Most consumers are not aware that many of the pharmaceuticals, over-the-counter medicines, food products, personal-care products, fragrances, and automotive products are exact copies of original brands. Counterfeit products are generally sold at a reduced price. Since there is no easy way for consumers to distinguish between the real and the counterfeit, the consumer (who generally makes the purchasing decision based on cost) is often deceived. In addition to the obvious legal and marketing issues (brand devaluation, market-share reduction, disruption of marketing plans), the counterfeit product puts the marketer at significant risk as a result of faulty product, unidentified health and safety claims, illegal and unsanitary manufacturing conditions. Counterfeiting is an indisputable threat not only to the consumer but also to those who are ultimately responsible for the integrity of their brand and company—the marketer and manufacturer.

Holograms, specialty inks, watermarks, tagging devices, and source tracking are some of the methods used to identify packaging and product counterfeiting. However, the use of these options can significantly inflate the cost of the product. Although effective ways of protecting products from being counterfeited are constantly being developed, there is no means of preventing knock-offs.

Consumers will generally choose to pay less for a product, even if they know it is not the original. The cost factor may be reduced when weighted against physical or health risks (food, pharmaceutical, and personal care), but ultimately even consumer education will not prevent these fakes from entering the market. Infringement and counterfeiting cannot be completely avoided. Packaging design professionals should understand the basic legal rights of protection and always consult with legal counsel.

RADIO FREQUENCY IDENTIFICATION DEVICE (RFID)

Radio Frequency Identification Device (RFID) technology serves to track movable objects. Through a decoder and a transmitter the RFID tag can read and write data. This technology has been used as a means of tagging animals for identification and embedding identification information into passports. As a tool for packaging identification, these chips are quickly replacing bar codes as a means of tracking pallets of products and providing data of product sales and shelf life. RFID is also used in packaging as a means to deter theft (as an item can be located) and at point-of-sale (checkout at the register).

Key Points about Legal Issues

✓ Make certain that the product contents are represented clearly and truthfully.

✓ Provide protection for the contents under normal conditions (from handling and distribution to retail and use).

✓ Ensure that the packaging is constructed with materials that will not have an adverse affect on the product.

✓ Promote consideration of the environment.

✓ Support the communication of the product contents.

✓ Protect the consumer from false claims.

APPENDICES

APPENDIX A Creating a Folding Carton Comp

MATERIALS

- Railroad board or 2- or 3-ply bristol: Railroad board and bristol are not the same materials as poster board. Do not let an art supply store tell you otherwise. Railroad board is solid white on both sides with pressed sheets of pulp in between; the exterior side is shiny, the other is dull. Bristol board comes in a variety of weights and is smooth on both sides. Papers adhere best to the shiny side of railroad board.

- Schaedler® Rule: This is a thin, flexible ruler with inches on one side and millimeters on the other. It enables the designer to measure three-dimensional forms like the circumference of a cylinder, the width of a bottle label, and the length of a structure to the closest hairline. This exactness is critical in packaging design since machinery and printing production require accurate mechanical files.

- X-acto® knife with #11 blades: Some designers prefer double-edge razor blades, but either way, practice and comfort using this sharp instrument is essential. These fine-tipped blades need to be changed often, so it is recommended that they be purchased in a large quantity.

- Number 2 pencil and pencil sharpener.

- Pushpin (not the same as a thumbtack, which has a flat head): A sharp pointed pushpin is used as a method of transferring the packaging die to railroad board.

- Scoring tool: Craft stores sell tools used for scoring. A paper clip (not unfolded) can work equally well.

- Straightedge ruler: A metal rule that is used to cut against.

- T-square: A tool used with a triangle to draw square angles.

- Triangle: With one 90° angle used with a T-square to draw against.

- Rubber cement tape or twin tack, a double-sided adhesive that comes in sheets: This is used on the glueflaps or tabs to seal the box closed. Double-sided or other commercial tape is not intended for this purpose.

- White 1/2 inch tape.

- Cutting board: A rubber surface that is self-sealing when cut on. The size should be large enough to cover the table surface.

- Packaging die: Usually printed onto vellum or paper. If printed die is not accurate, it's best to measure and redraw the die directly onto the board using a T-square and triangle.

THE PINHOLE METHOD

Getting Started with the Pinhole Method

Step 1, 2

1. Use white tape to adhere the corners of the railroad board to the cutting board.

2. Tape the top corners of the packaging die to the railroad board using white tape.

3. Use the pushpin to make a hole from the die to the railroad board at the end of every solid (cut line) and dotted (score) line on the die. When transferring this line to the railroad board, do not pinhole each dot in the line. A pinhole at either end is all that is necessary. The same rule applies to the circular corners of the closure: make as few pinholes as possible. Do not press too deeply; press firmly enough so that the back side of the railroad board feels like Braille.

Step 3

4. Flip over the railroad board a few times to check that everything is indicated correctly. Do not remove the die from the board yet. Once all of the cut lines and score lines are indicated on the railroad board, then take off the die and flip the railroad onto its back side.

Step 5

5. Connect the dots with a pencil and straightedge. It is not necessary to recreate the dotted lines to indicate the score lines. When the cut lines are cut away it will be obvious where to score. Make sure that lines that may seem unnecessarily a hairline apart (a top flap and side flaps are not always on the same score line since the top flap must fold over the side flaps) are indicated correctly.

Step 6

6. Once the folding carton die is cut out of the boxboard, the pencil marks left indicate the scores. With a paper clip or scoring tool against a straightedge, make a crease by running it firmly back and forth (do not apply too much pressure, and avoid scratching the board or ripping all the way through).

7. Once all the cut and score lines are lightly redrawn onto the railroad board, use the steel ruler and the X-acto knife to cut. Check the packaging die to make sure that it is being followed exactly. Go slowly and carefully using a sharp blade.

8. When all the scores are completed, the folding carton is ready to be assembled.

9. Fold on the score.

10. Use rubber cement tape, twin tack, or similar adhesive on the flap to carefully seal both the side and the back together.

Artwork and specialty papers can and should be adhered to the railroad board before the folding carton is cut out. This can be achieved using the same method as above. The packaging die should be printed onto vellum or tracing paper and placed on top of the artwork that is adhered (using twin tack or a spray adhesive) to the railroad board. Make certain to line up the artwork with the die using a T-square before beginning the pinhole process.

The pinhole method can be used for any packaging structure and material, from creating cutting labels to set-up boxes. Although the process seems time consuming at first, it removes the need for measuring every time a packaging die is needed to make a comp. Often packaging designs are presented in multiples, and the use of this method to transfer the die to the structure provides for consistency and accuracy.

If there is finished artwork for the folding carton, there are a number of ways to resolve the creation of the folding carton with the artwork in flat format. Since it is easier to be precise with measuring tools and straightledges on a flat surface, creating a comp for a folding carton is best solved when the boxboard is flat. If the artwork is in the form of a digital print, use a spray adhesive to adhere it to the shiny side of the boxboard. Place the die printout on top, making absolute sure that it is positioned so that all artwork bleeds appropriately and all copy is centered or lined up accordingly. Follow the pinhole method from step one.

When there are multiple layers of artwork, place the bottom layer down first (while the railroad board is flat and taped to a flat surface) and, using a straightedge, position the art elements and type. Check to make sure the elements are placed on a straight line and in their exact location. Rubber cement tape or another permanent adhesive can be used to adhere art elements to the surface. Twin tack can also be used to adhere printouts to the board surface. Experimentation with materials is always recommended.

Tips:

- ■ Measure from the center of a score line.
- ■ Scores should follow the grain of the paper or board, where possible.

Step 7

Step 8

Step 9

Step 10

Garyfalia Papadopoulou/ FIT (Fashion Institute of Technology)

APPENDIX B Packaging Design Portfolio

A packaging design portfolio should clearly reflect the designer or firm's capabilities and demonstrate an ability to meet marketing objectives, not reflect individual styles or preferences. The following are some guidelines for making an effective portfolio:

- Portfolios should speak for themselves without the support of someone to walk and talk through specific items, from how the book or digital presentation opens to the flow of the individual pieces. If it needs extensive directions and explanations, the portfolio will never be looked at. Time is valuable; therefore, portfolios that are self-explanatory and easy to navigate are greatly appreciated. If there are pieces that need explanation, then a brief description can accompany the work.

- Sample pieces should accurately reflect the work accomplished by the designer. Since most packaging design assignments develop in a collaborative environment, it is a given that not all of any one piece is completely "owned" by one designer. It is important to make sure that the piece reflects a significant amount of involvement on the designer's part. Check all confidentiality agreements to make certain the work is presentable and that design ownership issues are resolved. Packaging designs can take more than a year to get to the retail environment, and often the project gets shelved before it ever gets to market. In these scenarios it is important to get the proper approval to include work that may be deemed confidential.

- The presentation should be neat, clean, and organized, with no dents, bent corners, frays, tears, cut marks, fingerprints, or smudges. Images should be sharp and clear, cropped appropriately, and printed on good-quality stock. Digital images should be printed at a high resolution, color should be accurate, and style should be consistent. Organization of pages in a sequential format should be consistent in layout and size. Make it easy to navigate with pages reading horizontally or vertically, but not both, which forces the viewer to continuously reorient the portfolio. The best pieces should begin the presentation and then be scattered throughout. Save a great piece for last—it will make a lasting impression.

APPENDIX C Professional Sources

Note: Many of the businesses listed below have global offices. The offices listed below represent the location that provided contacts, images, and resources to the authors.

Addis Group Inc.
2515 Ninth Street
Berkeley, CA 94710
www.addis.com

Avon Products, Inc.
1251 Avenue of the Americas
New York, NY 10020
www.avon.com

Bergman Associates NYC
349 West 12th Street, 1st Floor
New York, NY 10014
www.bergassociates.com

BIOTA Brands of America Inc.
P.O. Box 2812
Telluride, CO 81435
www.biotaspringwater.com

BlueQ
103 Hawthorne Avenue
Pittsfield, MA 01201
www.blueq.com

Carson Ahlman Design
112 West 18th Street #5B
New York, NY 10011
www.carsonahlmandesign.com

Coleman Brandworx
35 East 21st Street #7
New York, NY 10010
www.cbx.com

ColorWorks New York
Clariant Masterbatches Division
130 West 25th Street, Suite 2B
New York, NY 10001
www.clariant.masterbatches.com

Cornerstone Strategic Branding
11 East 26th Street, 20th Floor
New York, NY 10010
www.cornerstonebranding.com

Crown Holdings Inc.
One Crown Way
Philadelphia, PA 19154-4599
www.crowncork.com

Cuticone Design
300 East 51st Street, Suite 14G
New York, NY 10022
www.cuticonedesign.com

Design and Source Productions
30 West 22nd Street
New York, NY 10010
www.dsnyc.com

Dean Lindsay Design
808 Chestnut St.
Wilmette, IL 60091
www.deanlindsaydesign.com

Flowdesign
200 North Center Street, Suite 201
Northville, MI 48167
www.flow-design.com

Georgia-Pacific Corporation
133 Peachtree Street NE
P.O. Box 105605
Atlanta, GA 30348
www.gp.com

Group 4
147 Simsbury Road
Avon, CT 06001
www.groupfour.com

Harkness Walker Design
16 Vardon Avenue
Adelaide, Australia 5000
www.hwdesign.com.au

Hornall Anderson Design Works
710 Second Avenue, Suite 1300
Seattle, WA 98104
www.hwdesign.com.au

Interbrand
130 Fifth Avenue
New York, NY 10011
www.interbrand.com

IQ Design Group
32 West 22nd Street #4
New York, NY 10010
www.iqid.com

Jones Soda
234 9th Avenue North
Seattle, WA 98109
www.jonessoda.com

Naturally Iowa LLC
1518 South 16th Street
Clarinda, IA 51632
www.naturallyiowa.com

Pantone Inc.
590 Commerce Boulevard
Carlstadt, NJ 07072
www.pantone.com

Parham Santana
7 West 18th Street #7
New York, NY 10011
www.parhamsantana.com

Pearlfisher
27 West 24th Street
New York, NY 10010
www.pearlfisher.com

Perception Research Services Inc.
One Executive Drive
Fort Lee, NJ 07024
www.prsresearch.com

Raison Pure
84 Wooster Street, Suite 703
New York, NY 10012
www.raisonpure.com

R.Bird
10 Bank Street
White Plains, NY 10606
www.rbird.com

ScentSational Technologies
425 Old York Road
Jenkintown, PA 19046
www.scentsationaltechnologies.com

Smith Design
205 Thomas Street
Glen Ridge, NJ 07003
www.smithdesign.com

Spring Design Partners, Inc.
126 Fifth Avenue, 12th Fl.
New York, NY 10011
www.springdesignpartners.com

Sterling Brands
Empire State Building,
17th Floor
New York, NY 10118
www.sterlingbrands.com

Toast Marketing & Design
325 West 38th Street,
Room 1410
New York, NY 10018
www.toastcafe.com

Turner Duckworth
831 Montgomery Street
San Francisco, NY 94133
www.turnerduckworth.com

Wallace Church
330 East 48th Street
New York, NY 10017
www.wallacechurch.com

Webb Scarlett deVlam
224 North Des Plaines,
Suite 100S
Chicago, IL 60661
www.webbscarlett.com

BIBLIOGRAPHY

COLOR

Albers, Josef. 1963. *Interaction of Color*. New Haven: Yale University Press.

Fehrman, Kenneth R. and Cherie. 2000. *Color The Secret Influence*. Upper Saddle River, New Jersey: Prentice Hall.

Wong, Wucius. 1997. *Principles of Color Design*. New York: John Wiley & Sons Inc.

DESIGN/ILLUSTRATION

Cirker, Blanche. 1962. 1*800 Woodcuts by Thomas Bewick and His School*. New York: Dover Publications, Inc.

Mijksenaar, Paul and Westendorp, Piet. 1999. *Open Here The Art of Instructional Design*. New York: Joost Elfers Books.

Volker, A., Kras, R. and J.M. Woodham. 2003. *Icons of Design: The 20th Century*. New York: Prestel.

Vrontikis, P. 2002. *Inspiration = Ideas: A Creativity Sourcebook for Graphic Designers*. Gloucester: Rockport.

Williams, R. 2003. *The Non-Designer's Design Book*. Berkley: Peachpit Press.

BRAND/PRODUCT/PACKAGING DESIGN

Angeli, P. 1996. *Making People Respond: Design for Marketing & Communication*. New York: Madison Square Press.

Angeli, P. 1988. *Designs for Marketing*. Gloucester: Rockport.

Blackett, T. and B. Boad. 1999. *Co-Branding: The Science of Alliance*. New York: St. Martins Press.

Datschefski, E. 2001. *The Total Beauty of Sustainable Products*. East Sussex: Rotovision.

Denison, E. and G. Ren. 2001 *Packaging Prototypes 3: Thinking Green*. East Sussex: Rotovision.

Design Library. 1998. *More Packaging*. Gloucester: Rockport.

Emblem, A. and & H. 2000. *Packaging Prototypes 2: Closures*. East Sussex: Rotovision SA.

Gerstman, R. and H.M. Meyers. 2005. *The Visionary Package*. Hampshire: Palgrave Macmillan.

Heller, S. and A Fink. 1996. *Food Wrap: The Packages That Sell*. New York: PBC International.

Hine, Thomas. 1995. *The Total Package*. New York: Little, Brown and Company.

Jankowski, J. 1998. *Shelf Space: Modern Package Design 1945-1965*. San Francisco: Chronicle Books.

Klein, Naomi. 2002. *No Logo*. New York: Picador.

Lubliner, M. and H. Meyers. 1998. *The Marketer's Guide To Successful Packaging*. New York: NTC Business Books.

Mason, D. 2001. *Experimental Packaging*. East Sussex: Rotovision.

Mollerup, P. Marks of Excellence: *The History and Taxonomy of Trademarks*. Boston: Phaidon Press.

Neubauer, Robert.G. 1973. *Packaging The Contemporary Media*. New York: Van Nostrand Reinhold Company.

Opie, R. 1987. *The Art of the Label*. Secaucus: Chartwell Books.

Opie, R. 1989. *Packaging Sourcebook*. Secaucus: Chartwell Books.

Phillips, R. 2001. *Packaging Graphics + Design*. Gloucester: Rockport.

Schrubbe-Potts, E. 2000. *Designing Brands: Market Success through Graphic Distinction*. Gloucester: Rockport.

Sosino, S. 1990. *Packaging Design: Graphics Materials Technology*. New York: Van Norstrand Reinhold.

Sutherland, R. & B. Karg. 2003. *Graphic Designer's Color Handbook*. Gloucester: Rockport.

Wheeler, A. 2003. *Designing Brand Identity*. Hoboken: John Wiley & Sons Inc.

Wybenga, George and Roth, Laszlo. 2005 The Packaging Designer's Book of Patterns. Hoboken, New Jersey: John Wiley & Sons Inc.

BRANDING/MARKETING

Baker, Susan. 2003. *New Consumer Marketing*. Hoboken, New Jersey: John Wiley & Sons Inc.

Bly, Robert W. 2003. *Fool-Proof Marketing*. Hoboken: John Wiley & Sons Inc.

Bozzone, Vincent. 2002. *Speed to Market*. New York: AMACOM American Management Association.

Feig, Barry. 1997. *Marketing Straight To The Heart*. New York: AMACOM.

Gladwell, Malcolm. 2005. *Blink*. New York: Little, Brown & Company.

Gruneberg, C. and M. Hollein. 2002. *Shopping: A Century of Art & Consumer Culture*. Ostfildern, Germany: Hatje Cantz.

Johnson, L. and A. Learned. 2004. *Don't Think Pink*. AMACOM.

Lindstrom, M. 2003. *Brand Child*. London: Kogan Page.

Neumeier, Marty. 2003. *The Brand Gap*. New York: New Riders Publishing.

Schlosser, Eric. 2001. *Fast Food Nation*. New York: Houghton Mifflin.

Solomon, M. 2003. *Conquering Consumerspace*. AMACOM.

Sutherland, Jonathan and Canwell, Diane. 2004. *Key Concepts in Marketing*. Palgrave Macmillan.

Zaltman, G. 2003. *How Customers Think: Essential Insights into the Mind of the Market*. Cambridge: Harvard Business School Press.

VanAuken, B. 2001. *Brand Aid*. AMACOM.

Van Gelder, S. 2003. *Global Brand Strategies*. London: Kogan Page.

Van Tongeren, M. 2003. *Retail Branding: From Stopping Power to Shopping Power*. Amsterdam: BIS Publishers.

ENVIRONMENT

McDonough, William and Braungart, Michael. 2002. *Cradle to Cradle*. New York: North Point Press.

Papanek, Victor. 1995. *The Green Imperative*. New York: Thames and Hudson.

Susan S. 1999. *Waste and Want: A Social History of Trash*. New York: Henry Holt and Company, LLC.

HISTORY

Meggs, Philip B. 1983. *A History of Graphic Design*. New York: Van Nostrand Reinhold Company.

INTELLECTUAL PROPERTY LAW

Bouchoux, Deborah. E. 2001. *Protecting Your Company's Intellectual Property*. New York: AMACOM American Management Association.

MATERIALS

Paperboard Packaging Council. 2004. *Ideas and Innovation*. Alexandria, VA: Paperboard Packaging Council.

Society of the Plastics Industry. 1990. *The World of Plastics*. Society of the Plastics Industry of Canada.

RETAIL DESIGN

Pegler, M. 2004. *Store Presentation and Design: An International Collection of Design*. New York: Visual Reference Publications.

Pegler, M. 2003. *Designing the World's Best Supermarkets*. New York: Watson-Guptill Publications.

Pegler, M. 2001. *Gourmet and Specialty Shops*. New York: Visual Reference Publications.

TECHNOLOGY

Brody, Aaron L. and Marsh, Kenneth S. 1997. *The Wiley Encyclopedia of Packaging Technology*. John Wiley & Sons, Inc.

Kaplan, A. 2004. A Touch of Glass. GlassTalk Archives http://www.gpi.org

TYPOGRAPHY

Berry, J. 2005. *U&lc: Influencing design and typography*. Mark Batty Publisher.

Bringhurst, R. 1992. *The Elements of Typographic Style*. Publishers Group West.

Gill, E. *An Essay on Typography*. Boston: David R. Godine, Publisher.

Haley, A. 1998. *Hot Designers Make Cool Fonts*. Gloucester, MA:Rockport Publishers.

Lupton, E. *Thinking with Type*. New York: Princeton Architectural Press.

McLean, R. *Thames and Hudson Manual of Typography*. London: Thames and Hudson.

Mollerup, P. 1997. *Marks of Excellence: The Function and Variety of Trademarks*. Phaidon.

Poynor, R. and H. Spencer. 2004. *Pioneers of Modern Typography*. Cambridge, MA: MIT Press.

Poynor, R. 1991. *Typography NOW: The Next Wave*. London: Booth-.Clibborn Editions.

Spiekermann, E. and E.M Ginger. 2002. *Stop Stealing Sheep & Find Out How Type Works*. Boston: Addison Wesley.

Tschichold, J. 1998. *The New Typography*. Berkley: University of California.

Carter, D.E. 1999. *Branding the Power of Market Identity*. New York: Hearst Books International.

Glossary

Acid Etching — A process of "frosting" glass in which the surface of the glass is decorated by dissolving it with the application of hydrofluoric acid to create a pattern or design.

Appetite Appeal — The visual means of communicating to the senses by attracting attention and creating desire for food.

Applied Ceramic Labeling (ACL) — A process where ceramic powders mixed with thermoplastic chemicals (which become ink when heated) are applied to glass containers by screen printing.

Agreement of Terms — A legal document signed by two or more parties that outlines a business relationship including the process, timetable and fees.

Alignment — The arrangement of visual elements in logical groupings to create visual harmony and support the logical flow of information.

Barrier Materials — Packaging material layers that protect products from the damaging effect of oxygen, vapor and moisture, aromas, static or the penetration of alien particles.

Billboarding — A visual means of creating shelf impact when the same brand of products form together to make for a strong wall of communication.

Blister Packs — The plastic, vacuum-formed, clam-shell structure that fits around a product and allows it to be examined.

Brainstorming — A thinking tool in which countless ideas, thoughts, impressions, notions are generated as a way to inspire new concepts and ways of thinking.

Brand — A name, a mark of ownership and the representation of products, services, people, and places.

Brand identity — The perception of the product of brand that can include all of the visual elements, structural packaging, advertising, etc.

Brand mark — The symbol designation used to identify the product.

Brand name — The word designation used to identify the product.

Brand promise — The company's assurance of consistent quality.

Canisters — A spiral wound cylindrical paperboard packaging structure manufactured in varying weights and lengths.

Category Analysis — An extensive survey of the product category to understand the strengths, weaknesses, and overall effectiveness of the competition.

Closure — The structural component that shuts the packaging.

CMYK — The term for the color model in which all colors are broken down into percentages of the 4-process colors: Cyan, Magenta, Yellow and Black for printing.

Color Management — A term that defines the consistent organization and uses of color throughout the design process.

Comprehensives — Also know as *comps*, these are realistic representations of a design in the form of a three-dimensional model or prototype used to simulate the final produced design.

Concept — The main idea of a specific design that serves to visually communicate a design strategy.

Concept Board — The presentation of visual elements that form the communication of the idea, impression, or personality of a particular assignment.

Confidentiality Agreement — A contractual document signed by an individual consenting to nondisclosure of all proprietary business activities.

Copyright — A form of legal protection that exists from the time original literary, musical, graphic, sculptural and architectural work is created that gives the owner the right to reproduce, perform, display and distribute the work.

Corrugated Board — The paperboard structure made of containerboard materials.

Counterfeiting — Copying or imitating with the intent to deceive.

CPT (Computer to Plate) — The production term that refers to the process in which the printer produces a printing plate directly from the digital files.

Cradle-to-Grave — A term that refers to the life-cycle assessment model of many products and packaging which begins with the gathering of raw materials from the earth to create the product and ends at the point when all materials are returned to the earth.

Debossing- The impression made by depressing an image into the surface of of a material such as paperboard, leather, metal, etc.

Design Proposal — A document that communicates how the project will be executed by defining the methodology and identifying the deliverables at specific points in the process.

Design Standards — A term that defines the acceptable tolerances and consistent uses of design elements throughout all communication mediums.

Die — The structural form used to shape, cut or stamp out parts and blanks.

Digital Printing — A process where all visual content is in digital form from creation to output.

Digital Work-flow — The use of technology throughout the entire design process.

Dust Flap — Flaps that extend from side panels that turn under the top and bottom panels that protect the interior of a folding carton.

Equity — A term when used in branding or packaging design that refers to the visual elements that validate the brand in the minds of the consumer.

Embossing — The creation of a relief, or raised image, on the surface of paperboard or other packaging materials by running it through a pair of dies in the shape of the image.

Engraving — The term for cutting a design into the hard surface of a printing plate used to carry ink in the gravure printing proces.

Environmental Factors — Consideration of the type and amount of packaging needed to ensure the safety of the product is weighed against what will likely become waste after product use or consumption.

EPS (Encapsulated PostScript) — A file saving format that can represent both vector and bitmap elements, and is supported by many graphic and layout programs.

Evolutionary Design — A term used in packaging design that refers to the minor changes made to update the appearance of a design without making a major, outwardly noticeable, shift in the overall visual communication.

E-tail — Retailing on the internet.

FDA — Food and Drug Administration.

Federal Food and Drugs Act — The 1906 act which prohibited the use of false or misleading labeling, was one of the first regulations imposed on packaging design.

Flexible Packaging — Structural packaging forms such as pouches, tubes and wrappers that are non-rigid used for an array of products.

Flexography (flexo) — The use of flexible rubber or plastic printing plates, similar to letterpress with a raised image area that carries the ink.

Flute — A term used for the structural element of corrugated board that provides strength to the material.

Folding Carton — A packaging structure typically designed to be a one-piece construction stamped out of paperboard or corrugated paperboard, scored (creased to be folded), folded, and tabbed or glued to make a structure.

Fourdrinier Machine — A paperboard making machine.

FTC (Federal Trade Commission) — A federal agency created in 1914 to prevent unfair methods of competition in commerce and now has the authority to adopt trade regulations that define unfair acts in different industries.

Glue Flap — The structural component of a folding carton used to secure one panel to the other.

Lithography — The printing process in which oily inks are applied to plates that carry the image and a print is made from pressing the substrate against the inked artwork.

Mandatory Copy — The text on a packaging design that is required by law.

Marketing — Planning and executing the conception and development, pricing, placement, promotion, and distribution of ideas, goods, and services to create exchanges that satisfy individual and organizational objectives.

Marketing Brief — A report that defines the selling strategy and objectives for a product or brand.

Net Weight Statement (Net Quantity of Contents) — The statement on the label that provides the amount of product in the container or packaging.

Nutrition Labeling — The copy on a packaging design that provides information about the dietary values of the product.

Offset Lithography — A printing process in which the inked image is "offset" to a rubber blanket that transfers the image onto the printing surface: the printing surface does not directly contact the plate.

Package — Refers to the physical object itself such as the carton, container, or bundle.

Packaging — Refers to the act of wrapping or covering an item or group of items.

Patent — A legal means of protecting an invention including a product, process, or business method that is new and unique from anything else.

Paperboard — A general term for the material made on a cylinder of a Fourdrinier machine.

PDF (Portable Document Format) — A file saving format that represents both vector and bitmap elements

PDP (Primary Display Panel) — The area considered the front of the packaging design.

Plastics — The origin of the word comes from the Latin *Plasticus*, and the Greek *Plasitkos* meaning to form, to mold, or to shape matter.

Ply — One of the layers of paperboard formed on a papermaking machine.

PMS (PANTONE MATCHING SYSTEM®) The established color system used throughout the creative industries that standardizes the color matching process.

P.O.P. (Point of Purchase) — A display designed to merchandise goods adjacent to a check out area.

Positioning — The placement of elements in relation to one another within a visual format. A term also used to refer to the placement and ranking of the product in the retail arena.

Pre-flight — The term that applies to the final inspection made to a digital file to verify that it is ready for printing.

PrePress — The process of preparing a file or material for printing.

Principal Display Panel — That part of a label that is most likely to be displayed, presented, shown, or examined under normal and customary conditions of display for retail sale.

Printing Standards — A term that defines the acceptable tolerances in color shift on the initial print run.

Private Label — A label unique to a specific retailer such as a store brand.

Product Analysis — An extensive survey of a product's primary and secondary functions including reliability, accessibility (how it opens and dispenses), optimal use of materials, use of shelf space, and ergonomic benefit of the structure.

Product Descriptor — The copy on a packaging design that explains the specific product contents.

Proof — A trial print used in the printing process to determine the need for corrections.

Proprietary — A term used in packaging design that refers to a design feature that is in the possession solely of the product's manufacturer and adds to the visual communication of uniquely identifiable brand.

Registered Design — A legal means of protecting the visual appearance or design of product packaging including a shape, ornament, graphic treatment (rendering, pattern, character), or configuration.

Registration — Accuracy of position to secure correct alignment of the printed color-to-color areas of a multi-color design image and of the design-to-scores shown on a die sheet.

Retail Design — The design of all elements of a retail environment ranging from the external elements of store frontage, fascia and signage, through to the internal elements of furniture, display, lighting, point of sale graphics and decoration.

Reverse Tuck — Top and bottom flaps on a folding carton that alternate so that the top flap opens from front to back while the bottom flap opens back to front.

RFID (Radio Frequency Identification Device) — A tagging device that electronically stores data for retrieval and is used to receive and respond to radio signals.

RFP (Request for Proposal) — An appeal by the client for firms to submit bids, pitches, or plans for working on a specified project.

Romance Copy — The copy on a packaging design that adoringly describes the benefit of the contents.

Rotogravure — The high-speed gravure printing process using a rotary press and wide rolls (webfed) of paper or other materials rather than individual sheets.

Score — A crease along the die of a carton that indicates the area to be folded.

Screen Printing — A printing process that uses a fine mesh screen stretched across a wooden or metal frame on which a design is created out of an impermeable stencil and ink is drawn across the stencil, thereby transferring the design.

Set-Up Box — A rigid paperboard box.

Slit Locks — Tuck flaps of a folding carton are slit into the top dust flaps for closure.

Solid Bleach Sulfate (SBS) — The term for the paperboard packaging material made of virgin bleached fibers in a single layer.

Spot Varnish — A printing effect that puts varnish only on a specified area of the printed piece.

Stock Packaging — The term used for the structures and materials produced in large volume available for non-exclusive use as product containment.

Straight Tuck — Top and bottom flaps on a folding carton that fold in the same direction and flaps that usually open back to front.

Swipe — A visual reference collected for a specific assignment and used as a resource for design inspiration and for communicating the visual essence of the product or brand.

Target Market — The ideal consumer group that a product or service is marketed toward.

The Three "R's" (Reduce, Reuse, and Recycle) — A socially responsible attitude on environmental concerns.

Thumbnails — Scaled down rough sketches quickly put down onto paper as a means of generating initial ideas, logo concepts, and layouts.

TIFF (Tagged Image File Format) — A bitmap format used for the exchange of images between applications; can be placed in almost all graphic and layout programs and is commonly used for the storage of an image.

Trade Secrets — The aspects of business that are confidential and not disclosed in the competitive arena.

Trademark — The brand name, logo, shape, color, and symbol or any combination of elements that can either individually or collectively be used as the means of differentiating goods or services in commerce.

Universal Product Code (UPC) — The pattern of bars used for electronically scanning products to identify the manufacturer and the product.

USDA — United States Department of Agriculture.

Value Added — A packaging design that provides an extra benefit of reuse to the consumer.

Violator — The term used for the visual device that is generally positioned on top of packaging graphics used for the purpose of calling attention to or announcing a special feature of the product or packaging.

Visual Hierarchy — The layout of design elements in the order of importance of information — defined by what is to be read or viewed first, second, and third.

Waste Management — The regulation of household garbage and the solid and hazardous waste produced by industrial and manufacturing processes.

Index